THE MEDIATOR AS HUMAN BEING:

FROM A STUDY OF MAJOR CONCEPTS OF SIGMUND FREUD, CARL JUNG, ERIK ERIKSON AND ABRAHAM MASLOW

by
HENRY A. CHAN

THE MEDIATOR AS HUMAN BEING:
FROM A STUDY OF MAJOR CONCEPTS OF
SIGMUND FREUD, CARL JUNG,
ERIK ERIKSON AND ABRAHAM MASLOW

by Henry A. Chan

ISBN: 1-55605-378-9

Library of Congress Control Number: 2005925236

WYNDHAM HALL PRESS
Lima, Ohio 45806
www.wyndhamhallpress.com

Printed in The United States of America

TABLE OF CONTENTS

CHAPTER I

INTRODUCTION

One morning, early in May 2000, I felt a deep urge to do something personally to benefit the lives of people in my community. By this time, anything I did in the community was as a clergyperson, as a priest or pastor. However, I now wanted to do something personally as Henry Chan and not as The Reverend Henry Chan. In searching my soul that day, I realized that one of the things that I wanted to do most was some form of peacemaking.

I know something about conflict in community. I was born and raised in Guyana, a country that was and still is fraught with conflict. The 1950's and 1960's were a time of great turmoil in race relations between the two major races, people of African descent and those of Indian descent. This racial tension was heightened when the native politicians exploited the racial differences for their own political gain. From then up to this day, race consciousness colors everything that affects relationships between Afro-Guyanese and Indo-Guyanese.

The division between the two races runs deep because both see that there is much to lose if the other has more power. Afro-Guyanese are descendants of slaves from Africa and make up the second largest population. The largest population is that of the Indo-Guyanese who migrated from India to Guyana as indentured laborers in the 1880's, about fifty years after the abolition of slavery in the British West Indies. The reproductive rate is generally much higher for Indo-Guyanese compared to Afro-Guyanese. Therefore, at least since the 1950's, the Indo-Guyanese has always had a majority in a fair election. The result is that the government in a fair election is always led by Indo-Guyanese. It would not be an unfair statement to say that the people who benefit most from government programs and employment are primarily Indo-Guyanese. Consequently, Afro-Guyanese feel disenfranchised, the result being ongoing political and racial tension and turmoil.

As a matter of fact, there have been times when the Afro-Guyanese have felt so frustrated over the lack of opportunities for advancement, that their energies have been released in behavior and actions such as strikes, racial violence and destruction of economic structures. The Indo-Guyanese are by no means saints. They use their political power to discriminate in an overt fashion against the Afro-Guyanese. The vast majority of leadership and decision-making positions are held by Indo-Guyanese. People of other ethnic origins who support the Indo-Guyanese government are seen by Afro-Guyanese as puppets and opportunists who speak and act according to the government line in order to gain special favors.

Today, the institutionalized racial hatred is manifested in social, economic and physical decay in Guyana, and this situation is worsened by a brain drain and a high rate of emigration to other countries, such as Canada, the United States of America and other parts of the Caribbean. Most of the people who are still in Guyana live only for the day because there is not much to look forward to in the future. For them, there is no reason for hope and optimism.

The local communities in Guyana are like those in any other country. People have their conflicts like anywhere else in the world. However, if the conflict is, say, between two neighbors of Afro-Guyanese and Indo-Guyanese origin respectively, it is not unusual for the race factor to be injected, even though in reality it may have nothing to do with it. One of the frustrations for me growing up in Guyana was not being able to do something to bring peace, especially seeing that I am not a member of either of the major races. Nevertheless, I yearned for real and lasting peace in my community, for at any given time, there was no telling when another explosive incident might flare up again.

Coming back to May 2000, the desire to engage in peacemaking efforts could have come unconsciously out of the unmet need to bring about reconciliation while growing up in Guyana. That particular day, I called the Reverend N. J. L'Heureux, Jr., the Executive Director of the Queens Federation of Churches, Richmond Hill, New York, and briefly described my thoughts. He suggested a few alternatives, one of which was community mediation, then gave me some telephone numbers to call. Of the several calls that were made, the only response was from Community Mediation Services in Jamaica, Queens, New York. I was told that a forty-hour classroom session was scheduled to commence in about two weeks. I immediately took the necessary measures to attend the entire session which included classroom instruction and role-playing. Following this, I had to observe at least three mediation cases, and then co-mediate at least three cases. All this culminated with a supervised observation of an actual mediation done by me. By May 2001, I completed the entire training and was certified as a volunteer mediator with Community Mediation Services in Queens, New York. Since then, I have also completed the classroom sessions for special education mediation, custody/visitation mediation and parent/teen mediation.

When I first started mediating, my primary focus was on the process of mediation. As I became more and more comfortable with the process, I began to reflect on who I am as a person, a human being, during mediation. As my experience as a mediator increased, I became more and more aware of what ties me to others involved in a mediation, that is, our humanity, our capacity for being human. As a human being, there are the physical, psychological and spiritual dimensions of who I am. This paper will examine some aspects of the psychological based on some of the concepts of Sigmund Freud, Carl Gustav Jung, Erik Homberger Erikson and Abraham Maslow. Even though these authors are no longer alive, they continue to have a great impact on the study and application of psychological theory today in universities and colleges as well as in the professional domain. Most, if not all, of these names can be found in the index of any textbook in psychology. The concepts of these authors are not mutually exclusive when applied to a human being. As a matter of fact, they are all simultaneously operative in each person whether they are aware of them or not, whether they are conscious of their existence and presence or not.

Note that mediation is usually associated with the legal profession. This is where mediation first started. Many books currently in print on this subject were written by lawyers. Today, however, interest in mediation is slowly developing in the cognate fields of psychology, sociology, social work, pastoral counseling and pastoral psychology. The use of mediation has now extended from the courts to the larger community and religious institutions. There are training institutions that prepare people to be mediators in churches as well as in private practice. Psychotherapists and pastoral counselors are beginning to see a linkage between what they do and mediation. Many see opportunities for expanding their work to include mediation. The reason for this is that people skills are pretty much the same in both disciplines. For instance, such skills as listening, reflecting back what has been said, etc., are used in both counseling as well as mediation.

Previously, mediators who were not in the legal profession were usually retired people who wanted to volunteer some of their time in the community. Actually, they were volunteer community mediators. Today, there is a trend in which people who are still in active employment, consider going into private practice as mediators or employed by an institution as a mediator, for example, a school mediator. Some school mediators are responsible for training and supervising older, matured high school students as volunteer mediators.

It is my hope that those psychotherapists and counselors who are considering including mediation in their practice or have already done so will find this paper useful. It is my hope too that those who are being trained or are already engaged in ecclesial mediation will also find this paper useful. The field of mediation as a discipline is still relatively new outside the legal profession. Previously, the focus was on the process. The mediator was seen as the defender of the process. But the other aspects of person and place are equally important. This study will touch on some parts of the person aspect, that is, mediators as psychological beings and their styles of mediation.

The next chapter, Chapter II, will consider some definitions of mediation as well as describe three major aspects of mediation, namely, process, person and place. These three aspects are all equally important. The different styles of mediators will be examined in Chapter III. Chapters IV, V, VI and VII will focus respectively on Sigmund Freud, Carl Gustav Jung, Erik Homberger Erikson and Abraham Maslow. For each of these psychologists, the respective chapter will consist of three sections, namely, a biographical sketch, a description of their major theories, and an examination of their theories in regard to mediators and their styles in mediation. Chapter VIII will conclude with consideration of some ways that this study on the impact of the various psychological theories on mediators and their mediation styles can be useful both to mediators as well as others in professionally related fields.

CHAPTER II

MAJOR ASPECTS OF MEDIATION

A. Definition of Mediation

Traditionally, the primary emphasis was placed on the process. However, the two other aspects of person and place can make or break the process in mediation. If certain factors in regard to person and place are not taken into full consideration, then the process is probably doomed from the start.

However, before going any further, it would be useful to define first what mediation is. According to Sharon C. Leviton and James L. Greenstone in their book, *Elements of Mediation*, "Mediation is the intervention of a neutral third party, who intervening at the request of the parties, assists the parties at dispute in finding their own way out of the dispute through equity through consensus."[1] Leviton and Greenstone explain their definition further by stating, "A less formal description of Mediation is that it is a process in which a neutral third party, called a mediator, helps disputing parties arrive at a mutually acceptable solution to their conflict."[2]

In their book, *The Mediator's Handbook*, Jennifer Beer and Eileen Stief define mediation, thus, "Mediation is any process for resolving disputes in which another person helps the parties negotiate a settlement."[3] The authors add, "In one sense, mediation is no big deal. People have been mediating for as long as people have been fighting and most of us pick up mediation skills from our everyday experiences. In another sense, mediation as a *formal* process has only recently become commonplace outside of labor and international disputes."[4]

Both Leviton and Greenstone, on the one hand, and Beer and Stief, on the other, have described mediation as a formal process. The first two authors also present "A less formal description," while the second two authors see mediation in another light, that is, "no big deal." I believe that these two perceptions probably have to do with the backgrounds of the authors. Sharon C. Leviton and James L. Greenstone are both law professors at Texas Wesleyan University School of Law. Neither Jennifer Beer nor Eileen Stief are lawyers. Beer is a professional anthropologist and mediator, and Eileen Stief is in the area of training and education in mediation. *The Mediator's Handbook*, was "the first mediation manual available to the public."[5] It was developed by Friends Conflict Resolution Programs, "A program of the Philadelphia Yearly Meeting of the Religious Society of Friends (Quakers), and is one of the longest-running mediation programs in the United States."[6]

In an excerpt from *Conflict Resolution Across Cultures: From Talking It Out to Third Party Mediation*, Selma Myers and Barbara Filner state, "Mediation is a process for resolving conflict in which an impartial third party assists disputants to negotiate an informed and consensual agreement for themselves. Decision-making authority always rests with the disputants."[7] In an article from Indiana titled, "Mediation," mediation is defined as "A process by which a neutral, impartial third party with no stake in the outcome assists two or more disputants to negotiate a voluntary settlement of their dispute, in which negotiations are usually conducted in private and communications with the mediator are usually protected by a confidentiality agreement."[8] Rob Scott of the Northern Virginia Mediation Service in their article, "The NVMS Approach to Mediation," states, "Mediation is a *PROCESS* in which an *IMPARTIAL* third party assists disputants in finding a *MUTUALLY ACCEPTABLE* solution to their conflict. It is both *VOLUNTARY and CONFIDENTIAL*."[9]

Robert A. Baruch Bush and Joseph P. Folger write in their book, *The Promise of Mediation: The Transformative Approach to Conflict,* "Across the mediation field, mediation is generally understood as an informal process in which a neutral third party with no power to impose a resolution helps the disputing parties try to reach a mutually acceptable settlement."[10] For them, mediation is an informal process only.

In the foregoing definitions of mediation, we see that there is agreement on certain elements. First of all, mediation is a process which involves three parties – a neutral third party and the two disputants who work towards the goal of reaching an agreement or a consensus.

There are some assumptions that underlie mediation as heretofore defined. Some of these assumptions or general principles of mediation are as follows:

1. Mediation assumes that people can resolve conflicts and are capable of discovering their own resources for doing so.
2. Mediators define and control the structure of the process but seldom make suggestions or give advice.
3. Disputants control the content of conflict issues and make the decisions.
4. Feelings and interpretations, as well as facts, are useful data in a mediation.
5. Mediators use the data in a flexible structure that they adapt to the context of each particular situation.
6. Values, beliefs, and attitudes are not the focus of mediation but can be discussed and may be useful in clarifying issues for both parties.
7. Mediation encourages understanding of and respect for other people's values. It does not require people to change their own values.
8. Mediation encourages people to choose options for resolving conflict based of jointly agreed upon and ac-

ceptable standards, without regard to the mediator's values.

9. Because the mediators themselves are committed to confidentiality, the disputants are often more open to the viewpoints of others and willing to take risks.
10. With the help of the mediator, parties generate workable and unique options for resolving specific conflicts.
11. Mediated agreements focus on measurable behavior rather than vague attitude shifts.
12. Participants in a mediation are likely to carry out agreements because they are personally involved in making the decision and have a stake in the outcome.
13. In a mediation, agreements are consensual. This equalizes power regardless of the background of the disputants.[11]

In regards to the first point above, "Mediation assumes that people can resolve conflicts and are capable of discovering their own resources for doing so," I would also add that mediation assumes that the disputants have a desire and are willing to work within the process toward an amicable and mutual agreement or resolution. I have seen many instances in which one or both parties in community mediation have the intention from the outset to take the matter into the court system, so they use the mediation process for data gathering on the position and facts of the other side. The mediation process will not work properly and effectively without the desire and full cooperation of both parties in working toward an agreement.

Jennifer E. Beer and Eileen Stief identify some circumstances when it would be unwise or inappropriate to pursue mediation. Mediation should be avoided when the following circumstances exist:

1. A serious incident has just occurred and people are

still too upset to carry on a useful conversation.

2. You strongly suspect one party intends to use the mediation to escalate the dispute (to threaten, to gather information, to look good in front of the judge, etc.).

3. One party seems incapable of listening to anything you say, or seems otherwise too disturbed to negotiate a workable agreement.

4. The main problem is, in your judgment, unmediatable.

5. You believe that one party might be better off using the courts or other forum. Power imbalance makes fair agreement unlikely.

6. The issue deserves public attention so that mediation does not hide a problem or a settlement from public knowledge (e.g. concealing environmental or work dangers; racial harassment patterns).

7. Key parties are unwilling to participate.[12]

B. The Mediation Place

Mediation takes place in a location, a place. Sharon C. Leviton and James L. Greenstone in *Elements of Mediation* use the phrase, "physical setting," instead of place. They emphasize that "the physical setting can have an impact on facilitating communication, gaining and maintaining control of the argument, reducing or increasing pressure on the parties, and insuring the safety of all those involved."[13] The two authors address some elements in the physical setting that need to be attended to, namely, choosing a site, arranging the office, and arranging the furniture.

When it comes to choosing a site, "Every attempt should be made to select a neutral site for the Mediation."[14] The guiding principle here is that the disputants must feel equally empowered, for "The perception of a 'home court advantage' for one of the parties could easily contaminate the process."[15]

Leviton and Greenstone provide a checklist for arranging an appropriate site for the mediation office, thus:

. Enclosed rooms with doors that provide complete privacy
. Sufficient insulation to limit sounds or conversations from another room
. Adequate lighting that is free of glare
. Adequate heating and cooling
. The absence of distractions such as ringing telephones or pagers
. Neutral or nonprovocative wall colors
. Adequate ventilation
. Adequate work space
. Minimal clutter
. Window(s)
. Wall treatments, window treatments, or furniture treatments that do not intrude
. Easily accessible restroom facilities
. Adequate accommodations for the elderly or handicapped
. Adequate security within or surrounding the office building
. A separate room(s) that can be used as a caucus room
. Adequate-size room for the number of disputants[16]

According to Jennifer E. Beer and Eileen Stief, arranging the furniture in the mediation room "will differ with the facilities, the number of parties, the degree of animosity, the type of dispute, the cultural background and personalities of the disputants."[17] The authors provide a checklist of major factors to be considered irrespective of whether there is a single mediator, co-mediators or a team of mediators. Those factors are:

1. Everyone should be able to see and hear everyone else

and participate easily in discussions.
2.   Members of one party should be able to sit together if
      they choose. Couples typically want to sit side by side.
3.   Everyone should be physically comfortable, undistracted,
      and feel as safe as possible.
4.   The mediators should be able to control the process.
5.   The seating should suggest mediator impartiality.
6.   Pick a location that feels comfortable and private: not
      too large, not too dim or cluttered.[18]

        Leviton and Greenstone and Beer and Stief all agree
that the best table to have in the room is a round table. This is
usually the ideal, for "All seats are the same, vision is unob-
structed, and the perception is that of bringing people together
and decreasing differences."[19] The next best table is a square
table which is indicative to the disputants that no one has an
advantage over the other, including the mediator. Should a
round or a square table not be available, then a rectangular
one will have to do. But the mediator must sit at the head or
one end of the table with the disputants at the right and left of
the mediator, so that they will be facing each other. No one,
except for a co-mediator, should occupy the seat at the other
end of the table. Irrespective of the shape of the table, all six
factors above must be taken into serious consideration.

C. Person of the Mediator

        The persons who are present in the room for mediation
are the disputants and a neutral third called the mediator.
While mediation cannot be conducted without disputants, the
scope of this study is limited only to the mediator. Much can
be said about the disputants such as their anger, ability to
manage conflict, ability to do problem-solving, etc. However, these will not be addressed in this paper.
        The mediator is expected to be a neutral third party.

The questions may be asked, "Who is eligible to be a mediator?", "What kinds of skills should a mediator possess?", "What kinds of personality traits should a mediator have?", and "What does a mediator do?"

Leviton and Greenstone in *Elements of Mediation* assert that "In principle, anyone can function as a mediator provided he or she is impartial and trusted by both parties."[20] Impartiality and trust in the mediator must be experienced in the disputants or they will be reluctant to participate in the process or cooperate with the mediator.

The mediator must possess the skills and undergo the training that is necessary for being effective in mediation. Leviton and Greenstone explain that, "The skills are learned in the 40-plus hours of classroom instruction, in-service training, and practical experience.[21] At Community Mediation Services in Queens, New York where I am a volunteer mediator, I first had to complete a 40-plus hour classroom training, observe at least three actual mediations, co-mediate in at least three mediations with an experienced mediator, and then be observed by a mediator supervisor in an actual mediation before being declared as experienced to be certified as a community mediator.

Beer and Stief identify some personality traits and skills of a good mediator as follows:

1. Strong "people skills," especially giving good attention.
2. Able to be directive and to confront.
3. Comfortable with high emotions, arguments, interruptions, tears.
4. Respected and trusted.
5. Imaginative in solving problems.
6. Patient as disputants inch their way towards resolution.
7. Able to empathize and be gentle, to withhold judg-

ment.

8. Impartial: putting aside one's own opinions, reactions, and even some principles.
9. Low need for recognition, credit, having things turn out your way.[22]

Leviton and Greenstone are more comfortable with relating how the skills of the mediator are reflected in mediation than in listing them. They write, "The talent is reflected in the sensitivity with which the mediator listens, hears, responds, empathizes, creates, draws parties into the process, and deftly maneuvers through the delicate and difficult moments with an intuitive sense of timing and appropriateness."[23]

Finally, what does a mediator do?" In the article, "Mediation Approach of Northern Virginia Mediation Service," the duties of a mediator are defined in this way:

1. Mediators provide a FORUM.
2. Mediators FACILITATE discussions and negotiations between the parties.
3. Mediators assist the parties to TELL THEIR SIDE completely so they FEEL THEY HAVE BEEN HEARD and so the OTHER SIDE CAN HEAR IT TOO.
4. Mediators act IMPARTIALLY regarding the parties and their dispute. It is the parties who will ultimately make a decision in the case.
5. Mediators use LISTENING, FEEDBACK AND REFRAMING as their main tools to facilitate negotiations.
6. Mediators use the PROBLEM SOLVING STEPS to guide the parties to:
   A) DISCUSS the problem and the parties' goals;
   B) IDENTIFY ALL THE ISSUES that need a decision;

C) BRAIN-STORM OPTIONS that might work;

D) EVALUATE ALL THE OPTIONS;

E) MAKE A DECISION TO USE ONE OF THE OPTIONS; and

F) TEST THEIR DECISION by applying it to antici-pated future events to see if it will hold up.

7. Mediators then REDUCE THE AGREEMENT TO WRITING – *using the language* of the parties and encourage them to return if difficulties arise in the future.[24]

Sharon C. Leviton and James L. Greenstone, in their description of what a mediator does, states, "The Mediator is primarily a facilitator who provides the parties with a process through which there can be a joint examination of the issues at dispute, an identification of common objectives, and in-sights into opposing perspectives. The mediator makes no judgments as to the merit of positions and renders no deci-sion as to which party shall prevail."[25] They identify nine roles that the mediator fulfills, namely, process facilitator, dis-cussion facilitator, clarifier, idea generator, face saver, agent of reality, messenger, distinguisher of needs from wants, and trainer.[26]

D. The Mediation Process

Generally, the mediation process consists of several stages that are usually standard. Jennifer E. Beer with Eileen Stief describe what they call, "The Anatomy of A Mediation Session." The session or the process consists of:

1. Opening Statement
2. Uninterrupted Time
3. The Exchange
4. Setting the Agenda

5.   Building the Agreement
6. & 7.   Writing the Agreement & Closing[27]

In the article, "Mediation Concepts," there is agreement about the above items. Stage 1 is the "Opening Statement." The second item above, Uninterrupted Time, is Stage 2 and is referred to as "Information Sharing and Issue Identification." The third stage that the article identifies is that of "Exchange & Negotiation" which includes the three elements above: the Exchange, Setting the Agenda, and Building the Agreement. Stage 4, "Agreement & Conclusion," consists of the last two elements above, Writing the Agreement & Closing.[28]

Leviton and Greenstone identify two stages in the mediation process. The first stage is the opening statement,[29] while the second stage consists of ventilation, information gathering, problem solving, and bargaining.[30] "Bargaining can only occur after ventilation, information gathering, and problem solving."[31]

This paper will use the four stages as described above in "Mediation Concepts," for it includes all the elements that are identified by the other authors. In order to provide an understanding of the mediation process, a brief description of each stage is provided.

Stage 1 - The Opening Statement

Beer and Stief, in a brief description of this stage, state, "The mediators—two are usually preferable to one—open the session with a welcome and an explanation of what will happen."[32] Myers and Filner assert, "The mediator discusses the process and describes the mediator's role, the roles of the participants, and the general expectations for the mediation."[33] The writers go on to say that, "This opening usually addresses ground rules that include agreements to allow each party to

speak without being interrupted, to treat each other with respect, and to allow the mediator to direct the flow of conversation. The mediator reiterates that most mediation sessions
are confidential."[34]

Leviton and Greenstone apparently feel that the Opening Statement is of great importance as it establishes the setting for the work that lies ahead. They point out:

> In the opening statement, the mediator lays the foun-
> dation for the operation of the session and begins to
> establish a rapport with the parties. When disputants
> choose Mediation, they often have an expectation that
> certain events will occur: the mediator will show ap-
> propriate interest in and concern toward them and
> their situation; the mediator will be competent to help
> them accomplish that which they have not accom-
> plished on their own; a structure will be in place to
> safeguard their emotional and physical safety; and an
> established, orderly process will occur that, if followed,
> will move them from where they are in the dispute to
> where they need to be. Parties come to the session
> hoping these expectations will be satisfied. The
> mediator's opening statement should be carefully
> crafted to respond to those expectations.[35]

With this background on the significance of the Opening Statement, the authors identify its purposes, namely, to:

- establish a safe environment to negotiate.
- establish the mediator's credibility and control of the
  proceedings.
- explain the mediation process and what will be asked
  of the parties.
- clarify the mediator's role.
- clarify procedures intrinsic to the process as well as

house-keeping procedures.

. obtain necessary commitments from the parties concerning their involvement.

. establish the integrity of the process.

. address the stress often associated with conflict resolution.

. establish rapport, confidence, and trust with the parties to draw them in as quickly as possible.

. obtain clear commitments from the parties regarding behavioral guidelines. Parties want to know that their emotional and physical safety needs will be protected.

. be sensitive to concerns raised by the parties.

. answer questions.[36]

The first thing that mediators must engage in to satisfy these purposes is to introduce themselves and then establish their credibility by providing information on their own experiences and credentials. The disputants are then asked to identify themselves. In regards to impartiality, "The parties must be convinced that the mediator is capable of acting as a neutral party and has no interest in the outcome. The mediator does not expect to gain benefits or payments resulting from the outcome."[37] Next, the mediator "should outline what the parties will do, what the mediator will do to assist the parties, and the scope of her authority."[38]

Having given their consent to enter into mediation, the mediator explains what would be expected of the disputants in order to keep the process moving. Ground rules are then outlined to ensure that the process moves along smoothly and with the minimum of interruption. The mediator must also assure the disputants that everything that is said in the mediation room will be respected with confidentiality. Expectations are also pointed out to the parties in regard to their commitment to the time required for resolving the issues, after which they are requested to provide their consent to commence the process.

Stage 2 - Information Sharing and Issue Identification

This is the data-gathering phase and from the data, the issues are identified. In the article, "Mediation Concepts," "Each party has an uninterrupted opportunity to describe the conflict from his or her perspective. The mediator reviews the major issues expressed by each party. At this stage, the goal is for the two parties to feel heard and for the mediator to identify the major concerns and issues to be resolved."[39] To this end, Leviton and Greenstone provide a more concrete approach, thus:

1. Ask each disputant to state his or her perception of the conflict. Hear all evidence pertinent to the dispute. Collect any evidence relating to the dispute, such as written contracts, cancelled checks, receipts, and reports.
2. Clarify issues.
3. Determine whether the parties agree on the credibility of the incidents and information.
4. If the parties disagree, direct them to identify the differences and encourage them to account for the disparities.
5. Clarify remaining differences and see whether the disputants can form a common understanding.
6. Ask disputants to determine what they want and what they need to resolve the conflict. Help the parties differentiate between wants and needs, because this distinction will be crucial in negotiating an agreement.
7. Listen actively to the disputants' issues and feelings as they are talking.[40]

During the information gathering and identification of issue phase, the mediator should listen to feelings in addition to the spoken word. Note that the mediator does not have to agree or disagree with any feelings or words expressed. Generally, all a disputant wants is an acknowledgement that his/ her feelings have been heard. In these instances, there is no material expectation. The mediator then must have the ability to reflect back to the speaker what has been said with the feelings that are associated with it.

Leviton and Greenstone propose guidelines for the mediator in respect to the information that is provided as follows:

1. Learn about the parties' interests and priorities.
2. Determine whether the parties agree on the credibility of the incidents and information.
3. Clarify the differences and see whether the parties can form a common understanding.
4. Ask parties to determine what needs must be met to resolve the dispute.
5. Help establish priorities among the issues.
6. Formulate clear goals.
7. Arrange agenda to cover general issues first, specific issues last.
8. Attempt to settle simple issues. Build on success.
9. Note overlapping interests of the parties and point them out.
10. Note parties' underlying needs and hopes. These are at the core of the dispute. Having them addressed and met will be the core of a resolution.
11. Reinforce areas of overlapping interests.[41]

The completion of this stage leads into the next which is Exchange and Negotiation.

Stage 3 - Exchange and Negotiation

Leviton and Greenstone also refers to this stage as the "Bargaining and Negotiation" stage. They point out that "Prior to the bargaining and negotiation stage of the session, the mediator took an active role in the process by gathering information and serving as a conduit for the parties. During this stage, the disputants must take an active role and directly communicate their needs and interests. This will create the psychological ownership that will make the final agreement work."[42]

In "Mediation Concepts," Myers and Filner describe the technical process of sifting through the data in order to identify issues that need to be resolved and formulating of criteria to determine the items of agreement. They state, "Issues are clarified and options for resolving the dispute are identified and discussed. In many mediation models, a brainstorming session about options for resolving the conflict is part of this stage. After the generation of options and without any attempt to evaluate any of them, the mediator and disputants develop criteria with which they will evaluate each of the options. The options are then reviewed, clustered according to where there is the most agreement, amended, and, finally, those options that best fit the criteria are selected to become part of the final agreement."[43]

Beer and Stief summarize this stage succinctly, thus:

While solving problems is not the only goal of mediation, it is probably the main reason the parties have come to mediation. The Building the Agreement phase is the time for parties to:

1. Identify and evaluate a range of ideas.
2. Negotiate with everyone's interests in mind.
3. Develop and test specific proposals.

4. Gain confidence in their ability to resolve the situation and to build commitment to the emerging agreement."[44]

Stage 4 – Agreement and Conclusion

The disputants initially entered the mediation room with a problem or conflicting issues. They have spent about an hour and a half or more and after all the effort that they have invested, they have arrived at the final stage, that is, an agreement. When the disputants leave the mediation room, the only thing that they will have to remember the experience is the agreement. The agreement will contain all the statements that they have arrived at through a meeting of the minds.

Describing this stage, the authors of "Mediation Concepts" write, "The mediation proceedings are usually summarized in writing. This summary, including the final agreements reached, may be confidential or part of a public record depending on the wishes of the parties involved. The agreements are written as much as possible in the disputants' own words, with the mediator playing the role of recording those agreements and helping to keep them balanced. Agreements are focused around behavior changes that are specific and practical rather than attitudes and promises to 'be nice' that only lead to further misunderstanding."[45]

Beer and Stief identify elements that an agreement should contain, namely,

1. Details specifics: who, what, when.
2. Is evenhanded and not conditional.
3. Uses clear, familiar wording.
4. Emphasizes positive action.
5. Deals with any pending proceedings.
6. Provides for the future.[46]

In regards to "pending proceedings" in the fifth point above, "If the parties are also involved in formal proceedings such as a court suit, a grievance procedure, a custody hearing, an inquiry, or a discipline process, the agreement should state what will happen to those proceedings. If the parties agree to drop a court case, make sure they know the procedure for doing so."[47] The continued existence of these proceedings could result in the other party having reservations about the future in spite of the written agreement.

In this chapter, we have considered the definition of mediation as well as the major aspects of mediation, that is, the mediation place, the person of the mediator and the mediation process. Next, we will look at the current styles of mediators.

CHAPTER III

MEDIATOR STYLES

In the case of human beings, if there is more than one way of doing something, it is inevitable that those ways will be tried and eventually one of them might be adopted as the norm. Mediators are human beings and, as such, the same behavior holds true for style in mediation. This study will focus on four mediator styles, namely, facilitative mediation, transformative mediation, evaluative mediation, and restorative justice mediation. The facilitative style is the oldest while restorative justice is the latest and applies primarily to victim-offender cases. In regards to the facilitative, transformative and evaluative approaches, mediators usually use one style most of the time and may occasionally utilize the others.

Before examining the differences in the styles, we should bear in mind that there are commonalities. In an internet article, "Different Types of Mediation Styles," which was published by the People's Law Library of Maryland, in considering the three most common styles of mediation – facilitative, transformative, evaluative – the authors state that there are three basic tenets which are the same, namely,

- The mediator is neutral (s/he does not take sides in the disagreement).
- The process is confidential.
- You and the other side determine the outcomes.[48]

These three basic tenets also apply to restorative justice.

Following are a description of the four styles, namely, facilitative mediation, transformative mediation, evaluative mediation, and restorative justice mediation.

A.   Facilitative Mediation

In her internet article, "Styles of Mediation: Facilitative, Evaluative and Transformative Mediation," Zena D. Zumeta, J.D., relates that "In the 1960's and 1970's, there was only one type of mediation being taught and practiced, which is now being called 'Facilitative Mediation'."[49] She goes on to describe what facilitative mediation is, thus, "In facilitative mediation, the mediator structures a process to assist the parties in reaching a mutually agreeable resolution. The mediator asks questions; validates and normalizes parties' points of view; searches for interests underneath the positions taken by parties; and assists the parties in finding and analyzing options for resolution. The facilitative mediator does not make recommendations to the parties, give his or her own advice or opinion as to the outcome of the case, or predict what a court would do in the case. The mediator is in charge of the process, while the parties are in charge of the outcome."[50]

The authors of the article, "Different Types of Mediation Styles," from the People's Law Library of Maryland, bears out the fact that the mediator is the guardian of the process while the parties are the guardians of the outcome. They write:

> Facilitative mediation is based on the belief that, with neutral assistance, people can work through and resolve their own conflicts. In a facilitative mediation, the mediator will take an active role in controlling the 'process.' Process means things like setting the ground rules for how the problem will be solved. The mediator asks questions to identify the interests of the parties and the real issues in the disagreement. The mediator helps the parties explore solutions that benefit both parties (sometimes called "win/win" solutions). In a facilitative mediation, the mediator does not offer

an opinion on the strengths and weaknesses of the parties' cases. The mediator does not suggest solutions.[51]

In order for the parties to reach an agreement, the mediator would normally have the parties in joint session and, if the need arises, would caucus or hold special meetings separately with each party.

In an article titled, "Mediation in England: Some Current Issues," Hew R. Dundas focuses on the strategy a facilitative mediator would employ to engage the parties without injecting his/her own opinion. The mediator would do this "by asking challenging questions (the conventional term is 'reality-testing') e.g. 'Have you considered...?' 'What if...?' 'What do you think about...?' 'What other options do you think might be available to you...?' and so on."[52]

Christopher W. Moore in *The Mediation Process: Practical Strategies for Resolving Conflict* says that facilitative mediators or "orchestrators" are non-directive and "generally focus on empowering parties to make their own decisions; they offer mainly procedural assistance and occasionally help in establishing or building relationships...and intervene primarily when it is clear that the parties are not capable of making progress toward a settlement on their own."[53]

B. Transformative Mediation

Transformative mediation was developed on the basis of a book which was written by Robert A. Baruch Bush and Joseph Folger and published in 1994, namely, *The Promise of Mediation: Responding to Conflict Through Empowerment and Recognition*. It was revised in 2005 with a new sub-title as *The Promise of Mediation: The Transformative Approach to Conflict*. The two key words which are associated with transformative mediation are "empowerment" and "recognition." Bush and Folger write:

This transformative potential stems from mediation's capacity to generate two important dynamic effects: empowerment and recognition. In simplest terms, *empowerment* means the restoration to individuals of a sense of their value and strength and their own capacity to make decisions and handle life's problems. *Recognition* means the evocation in individuals of acknowledgment, understanding, or empathy for the situation and the views of the other. When both of these processes are held central in the practice of mediation, parties are helped to transform their conflict interaction—from destructive to constructive—and to experience the personal effects of such transformation.[54]

The article from the People's Law Library of Maryland which was mentioned earlier elaborates further:

Transformative mediation is based on the belief that conflict tends to make parties feel weak and self-absorbed. Transformative mediators try to change the nature of the parties' conflict interaction by:

- Helping them appreciate each other's viewpoints ("recognition") and
- Strengthening their ability to handle conflict in a productive manner ("empowerment"). The mediator will intervene in the conversation between parties in order to call attention to moments of recognition and empowerment. Ground rules for the mediation are set only if the parties set them. The mediator does not direct the parties to topics or issues. Instead, the mediator follows the parties' conversation and assist them to talk about what they think is important. The transformative me-

diator does not offer an opinion on the strengths or weaknesses of the parties' cases. The mediator does not suggest solutions.[55]

Zena D. Zumeta also asserts that "Transformative mediation is based on the values of 'empowerment' of each of the parties as much as possible, and 'recognition' by each of the parties of the other parties' needs, interests, values and points of view. The potential for transformative mediation is that any or all parties or their relationships may be transformed during the mediation. Transformative mediators meet with parties together, since only they can give each other 'recognition'."[56]

In the article, "General Basis and Background of Transformative Mediation," Brad Spangler summarizes a list of ten distinct points of transformative mediation which was written by Robert A. Baruch Bush and Joseph P. Folger in a 1996 follow-up article to the 1994 edition of their book, *The Promise of Mediation*. The ten main points are:

1. In the opening statement, the transformative mediator explains the mediator's role, and the objectives of mediation as being focused on empowerment and recognition.
2. Transformative mediators leave responsibility for the outcomes with the parties.
3. Transformative mediators are not judgmental about the parties' views and decisions.
4. Transformative mediators take an optimistic view of the parties' competence and motives.
5. Transformative mediators allow and are responsive to parties' expression of emotions.
6. Transformative mediators allow for and explore parties' uncertainty.
7. Transformative mediators remain focused on what is

currently happening in the mediation setting.

8. Transformative mediators are responsive to parties' statements about past events.

9. Transformative mediators realize that conflict can be a long-term process and that mediation is one intervention in a longer sequence of conflict interactions.

10. Transformative mediators feel (and express) a sense of success when empowerment and recognition occur, even in small degrees. They do not see a lack of settlement as a "failure."[57]

Note that the transformative approach is not only confined to mediation. It can be used in any interpersonal conflict, such as "family quarrels, neighbor differences, business conflicts or differences between employees on the job."[58]

C. Evaluative Mediation

Christopher W. Moore states that evaluative mediators or "deal-makers" "are often highly directive in relation to both process and the substantive issues under discussion. Generally, they are very more prescriptive and directive with respect to problem-solving steps, questions of who talks and to whom, types of forum (joint sessions or private meetings), and the types of interventions made."[59] Furthermore, they "are also typically much more involved in substantive discussions and on occasion may give substantive information or advice, voice their opinions on issues under discussion, or actively work to put together a deal that will be mutually acceptable to the parties."[60]

According to Hew R. Dundas, "The evaluative approach to mediation, where the mediator does express some opinion on the parties' respective positions, is perhaps at least partly derived from the widespread use in the USA of what is called 'Early Neutral Evaluation' (ENE) where, on it becoming apparent that a dispute exists, the parties submit their respective cases (in outline) to a mutually acceptable third party neutral, often a retired judge or an acknowledged expert in the relevant industry, who will then consider the outline cases and produce an opinion as to the merits."[61]

Evaluative mediators, therefore, are experts in the law which governs the issues that are in conflict between two parties. With their expertise, mediators assist the parties in conflict to:

- Assess the strengths and weaknesses of their legal or other positions and
- Work to achieve settlements. In evaluative mediation, the mediator controls the process and suggests solutions for resolving the conflict. Individual meetings between the mediator and one party at a time (called "caucuses') are a major component of evaluative mediation. The focus of an evaluative mediation is primarily upon settlement. The mediators will make their best efforts to get the parties to compromise, if necessary, to achieve a result.[62]

Zena D. Zumeta describes the evaluative mediator another way when she says,

Evaluative mediation is a process modeled on settlement conferences held by judges. An evaluative mediator assists the parties in reaching resolution by pointing out the weaknesses of their cases, and predicting what a judge or jury would be likely to do. An evaluative mediator might make formal or informal recommendations to the parties as to the outcome of the issues. Evaluative mediators are concerned with the legal rights of the parties rather than needs and interests, and evaluate based on legal concepts of fairness. Evaluative mediators meet most often in separate meetings with the parties and their attorneys, practicing "shuttle diplomacy." They help the parties and attorneys evaluate their legal position and the costs vs. the benefits of pursuing a legal resolution rather than settling in mediation. The evaluative mediator structures the process, and directly influences the outcome of mediation…There is an assumption in evaluative mediation that the mediator has substantive expertise or legal expertise in the substantive area of the dispute.[63]

Of course, a mutually agreeable outcome would depend on how much the parties value the knowledge and experience of the mediator.

D. Restorative Justice Mediation

In an article by the organization, "Restorative Justice Outline," restorative justice is defined as "a systematic response to wrongdoing that emphasizes healing the wounds of victims, offenders and communities caused or revealed by the criminal behavior."[64] Daniel Van Ness and Karen Heetderks Strong in their book, *Restoring Justice*, identify three principles that are the foundation of restorative justice. They are "First, restorative justice advocates view crime more than simply law-breaking, an offense against governmental authority; crime is understood also to cause multiple injuries to victims, the community and even the offender. Second, proponents argue that the criminal justice process should help repair those injuries. Third, they protest the government's apparent monopoly over society's response to crime. Victims, offenders and their communities also must be involved at the earliest point and to the fullest extent possible."[65]

Any program rooted in restorative justice must be based on three elements, namely:

a. identifying and taking steps to repair harm,
b. involving all stakeholders, and
c. transforming the traditional relationship between communities and their governments in responding to crime.[66]

Van Ness and Strong quote Howard Zehr who said that, "Mediation must be dynamic, taking into account the participants and empowering them to work in their own ways."[67]   The two authors feel strongly about the importance of the mediation session. They write, "But, clearly, the meeting between the victim and offender lies at its heart. These meetings give victims and offenders the opportunity to pursue three basic objectives: to identify the injustice, to make things right and to consider future actions,"[68]

In the "Identifying the injustice" stage, both parties tell their stories. They tell about the conflict between them. The key element in this is that "It is during this stage that the parties put together a common understanding of what happened and talk about how it made them feel. Both have an opportunity to ask questions of the other, the victim can speak about the personal dimensions of the victimization and loss, and the offender has a chance to express remorse."[69]

The second stage in the mediation process is "to make things right—to restore equity."[70]   The specific aim of this stage is "to identify the nature and extent of the victim's loss and to explore how the offender might begin to repair the harm caused by the criminal act."[71]

Stage three has to do with looking to the future. In this stage, "Agreements are made concerning restitution schedules, follow-up meetings and monitoring procedures…"[72]

In evaluating the mediation style of restorative justice, Van Ness and Strong see many benefits and advantages. They conclude with these words:

Victims are able to confront the offender, express their feelings, ask questions and have a direct role in determining the sentence. Offenders are given the opportunity to take responsibility for their actions and make amends to the victim. Often offenders have not understood the effect their actions had on their victims, and the process gives them greater insight into the harm they caused as well as an opportunity to repair the damage. Both victim and offender are confronted with the other as a *person* rather than a faceless antagonistic force, permitting them to gain a greater understanding of the crime, of the other person's circumstances of what it will take to make things right. Several studies have concluded that victims and offenders who go through the mediation process are more likely to feel justice has been done than are those who simply progressed through the criminal justice system. Other studies have found higher rates of completed restitution and reduced future criminal activity by the offender.[73]

SUMMARY OF MEDIATOR STYLES

From the foregoing descriptions of facilitative mediation, transformative mediation, evaluative mediation and restorative justice mediation, the summary of each mediator style is derived from the duties and expectations of the mediator in each mediation setting. These duties and expectations are the elements that constitute the role of the mediator. The elements for each mediator style can be summarized as follows:

A. Facilitative Mediation

1. Controls the process.

2. Encourage parties not to focus on the strengths and weaknesses of their case but on their own goals and interests.

3. Asks questions that are oriented around problem-solving to enable the parties to arrive at their own agreements.

B. Transformative Mediation

1. Explains the main objectives of mediation which are empowerment and recognition.

2. Accepts responsibility for the outcomes with the parties.

3. Avoids being judgmental about the parties' views and decisions.

4. Adopts an optimistic outlook in respect to the parties' abilities and intentions.

5. Gives permission and is responsive to the parties' display of emotions.

6. Makes allowance for and seeks to clarify the parties' uncertainties.

7. Always be mindful of what is going on in the process of the mediation.

8. Acknowledges any statements made by the parties regarding the past.

9. Is mindful that conflict is complex and might be solved over a long-term process and that mediation is only one approach in conflict resolution.

10. Celebrates whenever there is empowerment and recognition, no matter how small they may be.

C. Evaluative Mediation

1. Controls the process and the outcome.

2. Focus by the mediator on his/her own evaluation of

how the case will be decided by identifying the weak elements in the case of each side, then, caucusing with each party to work toward a negotiated settlement.
3. Identifies options and suggests that the parties decide on a particular solution.

D. Restorative Justice Mediation

1. Encourage looking at crime, not as a criminal justice issue only, but as a community issue as well.
2. Focus on the harm done to the victim and the community.
3. Provide a conflict resolution process that is perceived as fair by both victim and offender.
4. Ensure that meeting between victim and offender pursue three objectives: to identify justice, to make things right, and to consider future actions.
5. Enable the offender to assume responsibility for own actions and the resulting harm and to repair the latter.
6. Seeks redress for victims.
7. Seeks to restore both victim and offender as full participating members of the community.

Next, some major psychological concepts of each of the authors – Sigmund Freud, Carl Gustav Jung, Erik Homberger Erikson and Abraham Maslow – will be examined to see how they inform us on mediators as persons as well as the styles of mediators.

CHAPTER IV

SIGMUND FREUD

A. LIFE AND TIMES

Sigmund Freud was born on May 6, 1856 in Freiberg, Moravia, which is known today as the Czech Republic.[74] He was the eldest of eight children born to middle-class Jewish parents, Jacob Freud, a wool merchant, and his second wife, Amalia Nathanson.[75] Freud's original name was Sigismund Schlomo Freud, but later shortened it to Sigmund Freud. There is not much that is known of Freud's early life as he twice destroyed his personal papers, once in 1885 and again in 1907.[76]

Freud's parents moved their family to Vienna, Austria in 1859 when he was three years old, and he lived there until he was forced to flee to England because of the Nazi invasion of his homeland in 1938.[77] Freud was a brilliant child who was always at the head of his class. In 1873, he entered the University of Vienna to study medicine when he was seventeen years old.[78] He was a dedicated student who believed in the theory of evolution and the natural sciences. This is no wonder, for according to Calvin S. Hall in *A Primer of Freudian Psychology*,

> Freud's long life, from 1856 to 1939, spans one of the most creative periods in the history of science. The same year that the three-year-old Freud was taken by his family to Vienna saw the publication of Charles Darwin's *Origin of Species*. This book was destined to revolutionize man's conception of man. Before Darwin, man was set apart from the rest of the animal

kingdom by virtue of his having a soul. The evolutionary doctrine made man a part of nature, an animal among other animals. The acceptance of this radical view meant that the study of man could proceed along naturalistic lines. Man became an object of scientific study, no different, save in complexity, from other forms of life.

The year following the publication of the *Origin of Species*, when Freud was four years old, Gustav Fechner founded the science of psychology. This great German scientist and philosopher of the nineteenth century demonstrated in 1860 that mind could be studied scientifically and that it could be measured quantitatively. Psychology took its place among the other natural sciences.

These two men, Darwin and Fechner, had a tremendous impact upon the intellectual development of Freud as they did upon so many other young men of that period.[79]

Freud studied medicine under Dr. Josef Breuer, a Viennese physician, who had treated patients with hysteria. During his association with Dr. Breuer, he became involved in a case that is referred to as Anna O., a patient of Dr. Breuer from 1880 to 1882. Anna O. suffered from hysteria and was eventually healed through hypnotism. This work resulted in a book by Breuer and Freud in 1895 titled, *Studies in Hysteria*.[80] Freud graduated from the medical school at the University of Vienna, in 1881 and later decided to specialize in neurology, the study and treatment of disorders of the nervous system.

In 1885, Freud went to Paris to study under a well-known neurologist named Jean-Martin Charcot. Charcot, like

Breuer, worked with patients who suffered from hysteria. Among the people whom Dr. Charcot worked with, some appeared to be paralyzed, but they actually had no physical defects. Charcot "demonstrated that such paralyses could be cured, and then artificially produced again, by hypnotic suggestion."[81]

About Freud, Dr. C. George Boeree says that, "After spending a short time as a resident in neurology and director of a children's ward in Berlin, he came back to Vienna, married his fiancée of many years Martha Bernays, and set up a practice in neuropsychiatry, with the help of Josef Breuer."[82]

Sigmund Freud was a prolific author and lectured extensively as he maintained his practice in neuropsychiatry. His works include *Studies in Hysteria* (1895) with Josef Breuer, *The Interpretation of Dreams* (1900), *The Psychopathology of Everyday Life* (1901), *Three Essays on the Theory of Sexuality* (1905), *Jokes and Their Relation to the Unconscious* (1905), *Fragment of An Analysis of A Case of Hysteria* (1905), *Totem and Taboo* (1913), *Group Psychology and the Analysis of the Ego* (1921), *The Ego and the Id* (1923), *The Future of An Illusion* (1927), *Civilization and Its Discontents* (1930), and *Moses and Monotheism* (1939).

Dr. Boeree states, "Freud's books and lectures brought him both fame and ostracism from the mainstream of the medical community. He drew around him a number of very bright sympathizers who became the core of the psychoanalytic movement. Unfortunately, Freud had a penchant for rejecting people who did not totally agree with him. Some separated from him on friendly terms; others did not, and went on to found competing schools of thought."[83]   Two of his followers who separated from Freud and went on to found competing schools of thought were Alfred Adler and Carl Gustav Jung.

In 1923, Sigmund Freud became aware that he had cancer of the mouth.[84]   He continued his work, even though the cancer made working increasingly difficult. Freud migrated with his wife and family in 1938, just before the Second World War, because Vienna was becoming a very dangerous place, for Jews were persecuted there by the Nazi invaders. Freud, being a Jew, and a famous one too, saw no alternative but to flee for his life. He died in England on September 23, 1939 of the cancer that had plagued his life for almost twenty years.[85]

B. CONCEPTS OF PSYCHOLOGY

Following are some of the major psychological concepts that are part of the legacy that Freud has left us.

1. The Id, the Ego and the Superego

Writing in *A Primer of Freudian Psychology*, Calvin S. Hall states, "The total personality as conceived by Freud consists of three major systems. These are called the *id*, the *ego*, and the *superego*. In the mentally healthy person, these three systems form a unified and harmonious organization. By working together co-operatively they enable the individual to carry on efficient and satisfying transactions with his environment."[86] When these three elements are working together, that person's basic needs and wishes are fulfilled. When they are in conflict with each other, that person is maladjusted.

Dr. C. George Boeree writes, "A part—a very important—of the organism is the nervous system, which has as one of its characteristics a sensitivity to the organism's needs. At birth, that nervous system is little more than that of any other animal, an 'it' or **id**. The nervous system, as id, translates the organism's needs into motivational forces called...**instincts** or **drives**. Freud also called them **wishes**."[87] The id has "its motivational impetus centered in the *plea-*

sure-principle."[88] Dr. Boeree explains, "Just picture the hungry infant, screaming itself blue. It doesn't 'know' what it wants in any adult sense; it just knows that it wants it and it wants it now. The infant, in the Freudian view, is pure, or nearly pure id."[89]

During a child's first year, "some of the id becomes **ego**."[90] Freud differentiates between the two when he writes, "The ego represents what may be called reason and common sense, in contrast to the id, which contains the passions."[91] The ego "searches for objects to satisfy the wishes that id creates to represent the organism's needs."[92] In other words, the ego is the *reality-principle* as the individual infant begins to discover the unpleasantness of the otherness, separateness, and outsideness of the real world."[93]

However, an interesting dynamic develops between the ego and the id, for

> as the ego struggles to keep the id (and, ultimately, the organism) happy, it meets with obstacles in the world. It occasionally meets with objects that actually assist it in attaining its goals. And it keeps a record of these obstacles and aides. In particular, it keeps track of the rewards and punishments meted out by two of the most influential objects in the world of the child – mom and dad. This record of things to avoid and strategies to take becomes **superego**…

> There are two aspects to the superego: One is the **conscience,** which is an internalization of punishments and warnings. The other is called the **ego ideal**. It derives from rewards and positive models presented to the child. The conscience and ego ideal communicate their requirements to the ego with feelings like pride, shame, and guilt.[94]

Boeree concludes, "You see, the superego represents society, and society often wants nothing better than to have you never satisfy your needs at all!"[95] The superego "constitutes the source of the human feelings of guilt…The super-ego is the projection of society's self-image into such an exalted state as to elicit devotion and adoration."[96]

In describing the inter-relationship of these three elements, Dr. John H. Morgan explains that, "the id begins necessarily to develop a negotiating capability—the ego as executor of libidinal powers—whereby the desires of the id are pacified with substitute gratifications which are physically accessible and socially acceptable."[97] The ego is under pressure from the super-ego which is associated with guilt that results from "fear of loss of love" on the one hand and a "fear of punishment" on the other.[98]

2. Anxiety

According to Freud, "Anxiety is a reaction to a situation of danger. It is obviated by the ego's doing something to avoid that situation or to withdraw from it."[99] The ego, that is, the "I" can sometimes feel pressured when there is an imbalance among the three major systems. There is reality, as represented by the ego; "society, as represented by the superego; biology, as represented by the id."[100] Boeree explains, "When these make conflicting demands upon the poor ego, it is understandable if it—if you—feel threatened, feel overwhelmed, feel as if it were about to collapse under the weight of it all. This feeling is called **anxiety**, as it serves as a signal to the ego that its survival, and with it the survival of the whole organism, is in jeopardy."[101]

3. Denial

Denial, a defense mechanism, is the blocking out of

external events from our consciousness. Dr. Boeree says, "I've noticed little kids sort of glazing over when confronted by things they'd rather not be confronted by. I've also seen people faint at autopsies, people deny the reality of the death of a loved one, and students fail to pick up their test results. That's denial"[102]

4. Repression

According to Calvin S. Hall, "Repression proper (hereafter called simply *repression*) forces a dangerous memory, idea, or perception out of consciousness and sets up a barrier against any form of motor discharge."[103] Repression is another defense mechanism which is called "'motivated forgetting,'...not being able to recall a threatening situation, person, or event."[104] This is evident in the case which "an alcoholic can't remember his suicide attempt, claiming he must have 'blacked out.' Or someone almost drowns as a child, but can't remember the event even when people try to remind him—but he does have this fear of open water!"[105]

5. Displacement

Displacement is "the process by which energy is rechanneled from one object to another object."[106] For instance, "Someone who hates his or her mother may repress that hatred, but direct it instead towards, say, women in general."[107]

6. Projection

Calvin Hall states that there are times when there is pressure on the ego from the id or the superego. In order to relieve this anxiety, the cause is attributed to another person. He writes, "Instead of saying, 'I hate him,' one can say, 'He hates me'; or instead of saying, 'My conscience is bothering me,' one can say, 'He is bothering me.' In the first case, one denies that the hostility springs from the id and attributes it to another person. In the second case, one denies the source of the feelings of persecution and ascribes it to someone else."[108]

C.THE MEDIATOR AND PSYCHOLOGICAL CONCEPTS

If a mediator's task is to bring health into an unhealthy situation between two disputants, then, it follows that a mediator must be a mentally healthy person. Therefore, the three major systems of the total personality of a mediator, that is, the id, ego and superego must form a unified and harmonious organization as previously stated by Calvin S. Hall. These three systems must work together cooperatively in the mediator so that he or she can function fully in the task of mediation. This presupposes that each system within the personality is in balance with the other two, that none is dominant over the other.

In examining the criteria for the four styles of mediation, namely, facilitative mediation, transformative mediation, evaluative mediation and restorative justice mediation, many of them provide the ego with full employment. Control of the process in mediation, concentration on the interaction with disputants, focus on the inter-relationship between the disputants, guidance of disputants, enabling the identification and repairing of harm, maintaining impartiality, problem solving, being non-judgmental, etc., pre-suppose much greater activity and engagement on the part of the ego, the reality principle, than on that of the id and superego.

To maintain interest, passion and excitement over mediation, however, the id, the pleasure-seeking principle, has to have some sway. A person must enjoy what he or she does and this is true of mediators as well. As a matter of fact, this is even truer of volunteer mediators. If someone is a paid mediator, as is the case with most mediators associated with the court system, the financial compensation is something to look forward to. But the volunteer mediator has to have a different expectation in the form of compensation. It is the joy and pleasure that is derived from mediation. Speaking as a volunteer mediator, bringing peace and reconciliation into the lives of two tormented disputants brings a brand of pleasure and happiness that is beyond compare.

A mediator is not without a superego. At least, we hope not. In the mediation room, a mediator is guided by formal principles, such as impartiality, confidentiality and a non-judgmental stance, as well as informal principles which are embodied in the superego. The more a mediator is aware of the presence and operation of the superego, the more effective that mediator becomes. As human beings, when we are aware of where a thought or idea or action is coming from, the fuller and more effective is our humanity.

Of course, there are times when the three systems of the personality might be out of synch with each other. A problem on our job or at home or with a relationship can cause an imbalance among the id, the ego and the superego. Such an imbalance could result in anxiety at a level that might adversely affect the performance of the mediator, and, therefore, the process and outcome of the mediation as well. We may not be able to eliminate the problem in whole or in part, but being aware of its presence could minimize the impact of the imbalance.

There are times when the id or the superego might be dominant over the other systems. There are instances when the id is so powerful that the mediator becomes self-indulgent by directing the disputants as to what they should do instead of facilitating the process to allow them to arrive at their own conclusions and agreements. This is something that evaluative mediators especially have to be mindful of. The crucial question to be answered is this: "Are my solutions or proposed settlements coming out of the process or out of some selfish need to impose my will on the disputants?"

Occasionally, the superego can be more dominant than the other two systems and this could result in performance anxiety. The superego tells the mediator that he or she must assume full responsibility for the successful outcome of a mediation case and must conclude with an agreement. In other words, if there is no agreement, the mediator is a failure. When this happens, a mediator can easily forget that he/ she is not to focus on his/her own goals and interests. Instead, a mediator is to encourage the disputants to work on their own goals and interests. All that is said here about the over-powerful id or over-powerful superego apply to all four mediator styles.

There are four defense mechanisms that Sigmund Freud identified which mediators need to be aware of if they exist in their lives, namely, denial, repression, displacement, and projection. There are some vital questions which mediators have to ask themselves. Are there any external events that are being blocked out of my consciousness? If so, what are the reasons for them? Is there any "motivated forgetting" in my life as a result of an experience from a threatening situation, person, or event? As a consequence of any repression, is there any energy that is redirected by me from one object to another? Because of excessive pressure from the id or superego on my ego, do I attribute blame and responsibility on someone else instead of claiming or accepting personal responsibility for them? These questions call for personal examination by mediators, for the presence of a defense mechanism can prejudice the way they process information, and this can lead to the breakdown of impartiality and neutrality. For instance, take the example that Dr. C. George Boeree gave us earlier in respect to displacement in which a person, let us say in this case a mediator, "who hates his or her mother may repress that hatred, but direct it instead towards, say, women in general." If one of the disputants is a woman, the mediator may find it difficult to be impartial towards that disputant.

Note also that in the role of listener, the mediator may want to listen for any indication of the defense mechanisms in the stories of the disputants and reflect them back to the teller as a mediator and not as a psychologist. When a mediator reflects back what a disputant has said, that disputant may begin to rise above the defense mechanism and be freed to move towards reconciliation and peacemaking.

CHAPTER V

CARL GUSTAV JUNG

A. LIFE AND TIMES

Carl Gustav Jung was born on July 26, 1875 at Kesswil on Lake Constance in the northeastern region of Switzerland to the Rev. Paul Jung, a minister in the Swiss Reform Church, and Emilie Presswerk.

Jung had a very traumatic life as a child. He was about six months old when his father was assigned to another parish in Laufen. According to Calvin S. Hall and Vernon J. Nordby in the introduction to their book, *A Primer of Jungian Psychology*, "It was here that Jung's mother developed a nervous disorder, probably as a result of marital difficulties, which required her to be hospitalized for several months."[109] The authors go on to explain the consequences of this troubled marriage and the mother's illness and their effects on their son as follows:

> Jung's parents had marriage problems ever since the child could remember, and they slept in separate bedrooms. Jung shared a bedroom with his father. He recalls hearing the strange and, to him, mysterious noises his mother made during the night. The sounds upset him, and he often had terrifying dreams. In one dream he saw a figure coming through his mother's door. The head became detached from the body and floated in the air. Then another head appeared, only to become detached again and float away.

Jung's father was often irritable and difficult to get

along with; his mother suffered from emotional disorders and depressions. When these conditions became more than he could tolerate, Jung sought refuge in the attic. There he had a companion to console and comfort him, a manikin he had carved from a piece of wood. The manikin provided Jung with endless hours of ceremonies and rituals; secret pacts and miniature scrolls were hidden along with it in the attic. Jung carried on lengthy conversations with the manikin and divulged his innermost secrets to it.[110]

When Jung was about eleven years old, he attended a large school in Basel with students from wealthier families than his. As a son of a clergyman, he was not privileged to many things which the other students had. For instance, Jung went to school with shoes that were well-worn out and things like these made him envious of the other students.

Later on, Jung developed a dislike for school and neuroses were developed from this. When he overheard his father's deep concern for his future in a conversation with someone else and his father's lack of money, Jung eventually became aware of what was going on and he immediately absorbed himself making up lost ground in his regular studies.

There are many psychic experiences which Jung went through as a child and, unfortunately, he had no one to talk to about them. The subject of religion was a source of great struggle for him, and the sad thing about his life situation is that he had a very bad relationship with his father. Consequently, even though his father was a pastor, Jung did not feel comfortable enough to communicate his inner struggles and difficulties concerning religion with him, for any attempt to do so only ended in increased tension and conflict.

Shortly after celebrating his sixteenth birthday, some favorable changes began to take place in Jung's life, for:

...the religious dilemma was slowly displaced by other interests, especially philosophy. The thoughts of the Greek philosophers attracted Jung, but his favorite was Schopenhauer, who dealt with suffering, confusion, passion, and evil. Here at last, Jung thought, was a philosopher courageous enough to confess that not all of the fundaments of the universe are for the best. Schopenhauer depicted life as he saw it, and he did not camouflage the undesirable features of humanity. This philosophical message gave Jung a fresh perspective on life.[111]

Anyway, Jung read extensively on topics which were not even part of his academic assignment in school. The breadth of his knowledge increased greatly and this would be reflected in his writings later on.

When the time was near for graduation from high school, Jung had a difficult time deciding on a field of study. "The concrete facts of science attracted him, but so did comparative religion and philosophy. One of his uncles strongly encouraged theology, but Jung's father dissuaded him from that choice."[112] Eventually, science was chosen and "soon after he began attending classes it suddenly occurred to Jung that he could study medicine."[113] He explains why he did not entertain the possibility of studying medicine earlier in this way:

> Strangely enough, this had never occurred to me before, although my paternal grandfather, of whom I had heard so much, had been a doctor. Indeed, for that very reason I had a certain resistance to this profession. "Only don't imitate," was my motto. But now I told myself that the study of medicine at least began with scientific subjects. To that extent I would be doing what I wanted.[114]

Incidentally, Jung had been named after the same grandfather who also taught medicine in the university which he attended. Jung's father died while he was still a student at the university and he was able to continue his studies with financial support from other members of his family.

After graduation, Jung did not waste any time in finding a job. He became an assistant at the Burgholzli Mental Hospital in Zurich on December 10, 1900. He was very happy to move to Zurich, for it is there that he began to establish his own identity. He began his new job with much drive and enthusiasm. He was determined to learn as much as he could about psychiatry and to learn it fast. He had a deep desire to help people who were mentally ill and the only way he saw himself doing this was to be as competent as he possibly could in his field of endeavor. He tells us how he went about accomplishing his goal:

> For six months I locked myself within the monastic walls in order to get accustomed to the life and spirit of the asylum, and I read through fifty volumes of the *Allgemeine Zeitschrift fur Psychiatrie* from its very beginnings, in order to acquaint myself with the psychiatric mentality. I wanted to know how the human mind reacted to the sight of its own destruction, for psychiatry seemed to me an articulate expression of that biological reaction which seizes upon the so-called healthy mind in the presence of mental illness.[115]

Carl Jung acquired much insight into the whole psychoanalytic process as well as about the therapist-patient relationship while he was at Burgholzli. It was during this period that he became interested in Freud, "especially because of his fundamental researches into the psychology of hysteria and of dreams."[116]

Jung became a lecturer in psychiatry at the University

of Zurich in 1905. He was also the senior physician in the Psychiatric Clinic for four years, then, gave it up because of an increasing workload from a private practice. Jung continued, however, to lecture on psychopathology, the foundations of Freudian psychoanalysis and the psychology of primitives along with other minor subject areas.[117]   An intense interest in Freudian psychology led Jung to establish a friendship with Sigmund Freud. This relationship grew and lasted for many years. But Freud made the mistake of portraying Jung as his successor. This was displeasing to Jung who was always independent-minded and had no intention of becoming prominent through the blessing of anyone else.[118]

The insights that went into Jung's works were not acquired merely from reading or from conversations with others. He also traveled extensively in order to learn about people in other cultures. He journeyed to places such as Tunis and the Sahara Desert; to Africa returning by way of Egypt; to New Mexico in order to learn about the Pueblo Indians; and to India and Ceylon where he delved into Eastern religion and mythology.[119]

Jung was a family man too. He married Emma Rauschenbach in 1903, and "she collaborated with him in his work until her death in 1955."[120]   Their marriage produced four daughters and a son. Jung writes of the two major interests in his life, especially during the period when he was analyzing his own fantasies:

> Particularly at this time, when I was working on the fantasies, I needed a point of support in "this world," and I may say that my family and my professional work were that to me. It was most essential for me to have a normal life in the real world as a counterpoise to that strange inner world. My family and my profession remained the base to which I could always return, assuring me that I was an actually existing,

ordinary person.[121]

Carl Jung was well known, not only in Switzerland, but also in the United States of America. He made his first visit to this country in 1909 with Sigmund Freud when the two were invited to lecture at Clark University in Massachusetts. In 1912, Jung returned to the United States and lectured at Fordham University on the theory of psychoanalysis.[122] He was also awarded honorary degrees by several universities, including Harvard and Oxford Universities.[123]

On June 6, 1961, death claimed Carl Gustav Jung – physician, psychiatrist, professor, scholar, writer, social critic, family man, and citizen.[124] His memory and achievements continue to live on through the C. G. Jung Institute in Zurich, Switzerland, as well as branches in several parts of the world. Many have found mental health through Jungian psychoanalysis which is practiced by his trained disciples worldwide.

B. CONCEPTS OF PSYCHOLOGY

Carl Jung's research and writings on human personality applies to all human beings in general. Calvin Hall and Vernon J. Nordby in their book, *A Primer of Jungian Psychology*, present us with a good summary of the structure of human personality from *The Collected Works of C. G. Jung*. They describe personality and its various components in as least a technical manner as possible.

Hall and Nordby describe personality as follows:

> In Jungian psychology the personality as a whole is called the *psyche*. This Latin word originally meant "spirit" or "soul," but in modern times it has come to mean "mind," as in *psychology*, the science of mind. The psyche embraces all thought, feeling, and behavior, both conscious and unconscious. It functions as a

guide which regulates and adapts the individual to his social and physical environment. "Psychology is neither biology nor physiology nor any other science than just this knowledge of the psyche" (*Collected Works*, Vol. 9i, p. 30).[125]

They add:

> The psyche is composed of numerous diversified but interacting systems and levels. Three levels in the psyche can be distinguished. These are *consciousness*, the *personal unconscious*, and the *collective unconscious*.[126]

All three levels are present and interactive simultaneously in all human beings. None is less or more important than the other two, for they are all interactive at the same time. Each level will now be described.

1. Consciousness

In Jungian psychology, consciousness "is the only part of the mind that is known directly by the individual."[127] There are four dimensions to the conscious mind, namely, "(1) extroversion-introversion, (2) sensing-intuiting, (3) thinking-feeling, (4) judging or perceiving."[128] The ego is closely connected to the conscious mind and is the "gatekeeper to consciousness. Unless the ego acknowledges the presence of an idea, a feeling, a memory, or a perception, it cannot be brought into awareness."[129] A person becomes individuated or differentiated from other people "only to the extent that the ego permits incoming experiences to become conscious."[130] This depends on which elements in each dimension are dominant in that individual.

The degree of dominance of the elements can be measured by the Myers-Briggs Type indicator which is based on Jung's work, *Psychological Types*. This indicator "is a useful instrument in helping to get a clear description of your natural tendencies. It is a non-normative instrument of 126 questions."[131] This test "can be done by attending a workshop on the Myers-Briggs types or by going to a counselor or psychologist who is authorized to administer this test."[132] The Myers-Briggs test is useful, for it enables us to determine what our strengths and weaknesses are and to which situations and areas our temperaments are best suited.

David Keirsey and Marilyn Bates draw our attention to some considerations of Jung in regard to the interpretation of the types in each of the four dimensions.

> First, it should be noted that Jung did not say that a person is either one or the other of these four pairs. Rather, one can be extraverted in some degree as well as introverted in some degree, thinking in some degree and feeling in some degree, and so on.

> Second, Jung did not say that one doesn't change in the extent of preference for one or another of the four differences. As time passes one's preference may strengthen or weaken. Of course, it is not at all clear what Jung meant by "preference" other than that, for one reason or another, a person chooses one way of doing or being over another.

> Third, the question of whether these preferences are "inborn" or develop fortuitously in infancy and youth remains unsettled. Jung apparently believed the former, though his pronouncements are not very clear on this point.[133]

Gary L. Harbaugh identifies 16 different "people types,"

based on 16 combinations of the letters for the following types, namely: Extroversion, Introversion, Sensing, iNtuiting, Thinking, Feeling, Judging, and Perceiving.[134] They are:

ISTJ	ISFJ	INFJ	INTJ
ISTP	ISFP	INFP	INTP
ESTP	ESFP	ENFP	ENTP
ESTJ	ESFJ	ENFJ	ENTJ

Every person belongs to one of these 16 people or personality types.

2. The Personal Unconscious

Calvin S. Hall and Vernon J. Nordby state that experiences which are not recognized by the ego, that is, not being placed or retained in consciousness, are stored elsewhere. They are filed away in what is called the personal unconscious by C. G. Jung.[135] They write:

> This level of the mind adjoins the ego. It is the receptacle that contains all those psychic activities and contents which are incongruous with the conscious individuation or function. Or, they were once conscious experiences which have been repressed or disregarded for various reasons, such as a distressing thought, an unsolved problem, a personal conflict, or a moral issue. Often they are forgotten simply because they were irrelevant or seemed unimportant at the time they were experienced. All experiences that are too weak to reach consciousness, or too weak to remain in consciousness, are stored in the personal unconscious."[136]

Note that these experiences can be retrieved or accessed by the ego whenever they are needed. Examples of this are the recalling of names and faces of people and incidents from years in the past.

According to C. G. Jung, groups of contents may clump together to form a cluster or constellation in the personal unconscious and are called complexes.[137] For instance, a person may have an inferiority complex or a superiority complex which would have significant influence on his or her behavior.

Hall and Nordby also speak on the impact of complexes identified by Jung as follows:

> Further study of these complexes indicated that they are like separate little personalities within the total personality. They are autonomous, possess their own driving force, and can be very powerful in controlling our thoughts and behavior.[138]

Jung claims that complexes have their origin in the collective unconscious and may be developed personally from traumatic experiences in childhood. Complexes can be identified and resolved through individual psychotherapy.[139]

3. The Collective Unconscious

The collective unconscious consists of images which are inherited by every human being from previous generations. Hall and Nordby describe this component of the psyche in this way:

> The collective unconscious is a reservoir of latent images, usually called *primordial images* by Jung. *Primordial* means "first" or "original"; therefore a primordial image refers to the earliest development of the psyche. Man inherits these images from his ancestral past, a past that includes all of his human ancestors as well as his prehuman or animal ancestors. These racial images are not inherited in the sense that

a person consciously remembers or has images that his ancestors had. Rather they are predispositions or potentialities for experiencing and responding to the world in the same ways that his ancestors did.[140]

The two authors point out that many of the phobias of humankind are inherited and are part of the collective unconscious, such as the "fear of snakes or of the dark."[141] Put differently, "a fear of something can develop quite easily if the predisposition to feel fear already exists in the collective unconscious."[142]

Perceptions and actions which originate from the collective unconscious do have implications for many aspects of a person's life. Therefore, the goal in life is to bring as much of the collective unconscious as possible into the conscious through education and the accumulation of experiences. Calvin Hall and Vernon Nordby explain:

> The contents of the collective unconscious exercise a preformed pattern for personal behavior to follow from the day the individual is born. "The form of the world into which he is born is already inborn in him as a virtual image" (Vol. 7, p. 188). This virtual image comes into conscious reality by identifying itself with corresponding objects in the world. For example, if a virtual image of the mother exists in the collective unconscious it will quickly express itself by the infant's perceiving and reacting to its actual mother. Thus, the contents of the collective unconscious are responsible for the selectivity of perception and action. We easily perceive some things and react to them in certain ways because the collective unconscious is predisposed to them.

The more experiences we have, the greater are the

chances that the latent images will become manifested. That is why a rich environment and opportunities for education and learning are necessary for individuating (making conscious) all aspects of the collective unconscious.[143]

Consequently, a person can become adept in more aspects of life. The more opportunities for education and the broadening of experiences that a person is exposed to, the higher the probability that that person will be successful in this pursuit.

What are the contents of the collective unconscious? Carl Jung calls them archetypes. Hall and Nordby explain what the archetypes are:

> The word archetype means an original model after which other similar things are patterned. A synonym is *prototype*.

> Jung spent much time during the last forty years of his life investigating and writing about the archetypes. Among the numerous archetypes that he identified and described are those of birth, rebirth, death, power, magic, the hero, the child, the trickster, God, the demon, the wise old man, the earth mother, the giant, many natural objects like trees, the sun, the moon, wind, rivers, fire, and animals, and many man-made objects such as rings and weapons.[144]

It is extremely important that everyone understand the archetypes that are dominant and operative in their lives and appreciate their power, for they play a part in determining the extent of the fullness, meaningfulness and effectiveness of their lives.

Four archetypes exert a great deal of influence in "shaping our personality and behavior...These are the *persona*, the *anima* and *animus*, the *shadow*, and the *self*."[145] The more a mediator claims and embraces these archetypes, the greater are the chances for psychological wholeness and integration. The result, in this case, is increased effectiveness in mediation.

The persona is defined as "the mask or façade one exhibits publicly, with the intention of presenting a favorable impression so that society will accept him. It might also be called the *conformity* archetype...A person may have more than one mask...Collectively, however, all of his masks constitute his persona."[146]

According to C. G. Jung, an archetype that a person must be very attentive to in his or her psyche is the anima or the animus which is responsible for healthy relationships between sexes.

> Jung called the persona the "outward face" of the psyche because it is that face which the world sees. The "inward face" he called the *anima* in males and the *animus* in females. The anima archetype is the feminine side of the male psyche; the animus archetype is the masculine side of the female psyche. Every person has qualities of the opposite sex, not only in the biological sense that man and woman secrete both male and female sex hormones but also in a psychological sense of attitudes and feelings...Thus the anima and animus archetypes, like that of the persona, have strong survival value.

> If the personality is to be well adjusted and harmoniously balanced, the feminine side of a man's personality and the masculine side of a woman's personality must be allowed to express themselves in consciousness and behavior.[147]

Jung identified the shadow which "contains more of man's basic animal nature than any other archetype does."[148] Hall and Nordby advocate a balance between suppression and freedom of the shadow. They write:

> In order for a person to become an integral member of the community, it is necessary to tame his animal spirits contained in the shadow. This taming is accomplished by suppressing manifestations of the shadow and by developing a strong persona which counteracts the power of the shadow. The person who suppresses the animal side of his nature may become civilized, but he does so at the expense of decreasing the motive power for spontaneity, creativity, strong emotions, and deep insights. He cuts himself off from the wisdom of his instinctual nature, a wisdom that may be more profound than any learning or culture can provide. A shadowless life tends to become shallow and spiritless.

> The shadow is persistent, however; it does not yield easily to suppression…The shadow in this respect is an important and valuable archetype because it has the capacity to retain and assert ideas or images that may turn out to be advantageous to the individual. By its tenacity it can thrust a person into more satisfying and creative activities.[149]

To C. G. Jung, the self as an archetype is: "The organizing principle of the personality."[150] Hall and Nordby articulate on this archetype further:

> The self is the central archetype in the collective unconscious, much as the sun is the center of the solar system. The self is the archetype of order, organiza-

tion, and unification; it draws to itself and harmonizes all the archetypes and their manifestations in complexes and consciousness. It unites the personality, giving it a sense of "oneness" and firmness. When a person says he feels in harmony with himself and with the world, we can be sure that the self archetype is performing its work effectively. On the other hand, when a person feels "out of sorts" and discontented, or more seriously conflicted and feels he is "going to pieces," the self is not doing its job properly.

The ultimate goal of every personality is to achieve a state of selfhood and self-realization.[151]

Hall and Nordby describe the rich legacy that Carl Jung has left us when they write, "Jung's writings are an inexhaustible fount of wisdom and inspiration which one can return to repeatedly to learn something new about himself and about the world. That is why it is a uniquely enriching and refreshing experience to read Jung."[152]

C. THE MEDIATOR AND PSYCHOLOGICAL CONCEPTS

Carl Jung's research and writings on human personality pertains to all human beings, non-mediators as well as mediators. Mediators, irrespective of their styles, cannot avoid bringing their own personalities into a mediation room. They cannot check in their personalities at the door, so to speak. Consequently, all behavior and decisions of mediators are the result of their own personalities, and knowledge of the structure and components of human personality can provide them with invaluable insights into who they are as persons and why they behave the way they do.

Incidentally, each individual's personality is unique and this factor can complicate matters in the case of co-mediation. When two volunteer mediators are assigned to co-me-diate a case, it is possible that they have never met each other before the case and, therefore, know nothing about each other. I have been in a couple of such situations before and because of some goodwill on the part of the other mediator and me, we did manage to work cooperatively with each other for the good of the parties in dispute. However, there are times when it was not so easy. You know that some tension is there and you hope that the disputants will not be affected by it. Such a situation occurs, not because the mediators are bad persons, but simply because mediator styles can vary with personality type. Sometimes, a way of facilitating some adjustment be-tween two strangers who will mediate a case is to have them spend a little time to talk to each other and to agree on who will lead which parts of the mediation process.

According to C. G. Jung, there are four dimensions to consciousness which are controlled by the ego. These di-mensions are of the utmost importance because they consti-tute the basis, the criteria, that the ego uses to determine what data to allow into consciousness. The four dimensions are four pairs of opposites, namely, extroversion-introversion, sensing-intuiting, thinking-feeling, and judging-perceiving. Each individual personality consists of four components, that is, one from each pair. This is why Gary Harbaugh identifies sixteen different combinations or people types. Mediators can learn what their individual people type is by taking the Myers-Briggs test which can prove useful, for it would en-able them to determine what their strengths and weaknesses are and to which situations and styles of mediation for which their temperament is best suited.

Difference in types can have implications in mediation regardless of the mediation style. For example, the mediator and a disputant might be thinking types while the other dis-putant is a feeling type. I think it would be helpful if the mediator has an idea of his/her type as well as those of the disputants in this case. This would improve communication tremendously, for the mediator would then exert more effort into listening to the feelings of the disputant and respond to the feelings from the heart instead of from the head.

When a mediator, regardless of the style of mediation, has unresolved issues in his or her life that are buried in the personal unconsciousness, those issues could surface and have implications as far as the mediation is concerned. An example of this is the situation cited in the section on Sigmund Freud involving displacement, that is, "Someone who hates his or her mother may repress that hatred, but direct it instead, say, to women in general." To Jung, the hatred of the mother is repressed into the personal unconscious, and if this someone is a mediator, there is the chance of the mediator directing the hatred to women in general, one of whom can be a disputant. The impartiality of the mediator, therefore, would obviously be compromised.

Carl Jung states that groups of contents may clump together as a cluster in the personal unconsciousness, thus, forming what are called complexes. The presence of, say, an inferiority or a superiority complex in the personality of a mediator could have significant influence on his or her behavior in mediation. If there is an inferiority complex, will the mediator be able to control the process, regardless of style of mediation? This is a question that has to be resolved if the mediator will be able to function fully and effectively. If the mediator has a superiority complex, would he/she be able to encourage and empower the parties to pursue their goals and interests or will he/she impose his/her will on them? In the case of evaluative mediation, will the mediator constantly seek to dictate courses of actions or agreements which come from the superiority complex rather than from the process? In restorative justice mediation, how will the mediator with a superiority complex relate to the victim and the offender, especially the latter? Will the mediator exhibit self-righteousness?

Can a mediator be fair and effective when Jung's concept of the inferiority complex is combined with Freud's concept of the superego in his/her personality?

Our perceptions of situations in mediation are influenced by the collective unconscious. According to Jung, the collective unconscious contains archetypes which are dominant and operative in our lives as human beings. It would be very helpful if mediators appreciate the power of archetypes, for they also play an important role in determining the particular style of the mediator. Of particular interest are the archetypes of the persona, the animus and anima, the shadow, and the self.

There is a persona for the role of mediator. There is a public mask or façade which mediators wear. This persona is what moves the disputants to recognize the authority of the mediator. It is the persona that enables the mediator to be the protector and defender of the process.

Another important archetype is the animus in females and the anima in males. If the animus is not properly developed in a woman, she can have problems in relating to men. Similarly, if the anima is not properly developed in a man, he can have problems in relationships with women. We can see the implications these archetypes can have on the way we relate to disputants as well as co-mediators.

To some extent, the mediator needs to allow the shadow to express itself. The mediator needs to be flexible and spontaneous. The mediator must acknowledge his or her own humanity as well as that of the disputants. I believe that disputants expect mediators to show evidence of at least some awareness of their humanity before they begin to feel comfortable enough to participate fully in the mediation process. Disputants, in my experience, also expect mediators to be persons of insight as well as emotions. They expect them to be human beings and not robots in the mediation room.

Finally, the archetype of the self, the "organizing principle of the personality" is of the utmost importance. If the self is fragmented, the mediator will not be able to control the process or possess the energy required to enable or empower the disputants to work towards reconciliation and eventually to an agreement. A mediator who is "out of sorts," discontented with life, seriously conflicted, and is falling to pieces, cannot bring healing to the parties who, because of their conflict or problem, most likely feel fragmented too instead of integrated. This is why they come to mediation, to overcome fragmentation and obtain integration.

Many of our daily perceptions and actions in life originate from the collective unconscious and do have implications for mediation. The goal in life for the mediator, therefore, is to bring as much of the collective unconscious as possible into the conscious through education and the opportunities for expanding life experiences. This is part of life's mission anyway, that is, to know and embrace the self in fuller and, hopefully, richer ways.

CHAPTER VI

ERIK HOMBERGER ERIKSON

A. LIFE AND TIMES

Erik Erikson was born on 15th June, 1902 in Frankfurt, Germany. His biological father most likely was an unknown Danish man and his mother, Karla Abrahamsen, was Jewish.[153] His parents were separated before he was born. When Erikson was born, his mother was a single parent until she married Theodor Homberger who was little Erik's pediatrician. Theodor and Karla Homberger raised the child as Erik Homberger. While he was growing up as a young boy, Erik experienced some prejudice because of his Jewish faith and Danish features. He experienced an identity crisis. He was taunted at the synagogue because of his blond and blue-eyed Nordic features by the Jews, and ridiculed in grammar school for being Jewish. Friedman adds, "He never forgot the humiliation of being referred to as a Gentile in synagogue and a Jew in school."[154] His later work on self-identity could have been influenced by the results of these traumatic boyhood experiences.

Erikson had developed a disdain for formal education systems. Consequently, after graduating from grammar school, he chose not to further his education by going to a university. Instead, he studied art at the Baden State Art School, and whenever he had the time, he traveled around Europe.[155] His desire was to live a carefree life. In the 1920's, a friend named Peter Blos suggested that he apply for a position at a school for English American students which was run by Dorothy Burlingham, a friend of Anna Freud.[156] Erik Homburger taught art and obtained a certificate in the

Montessori education in addition to a second certificate in child psychoanalyses from the Vienna Psychoanalytic Society.[157] He "completed a training analysis with Anna Freud and had become skilled in the new field of child analysis."[158]

While he was a teacher, Erik Homberger met and later married Joan Serson who was a physical education and English teacher at the same school where he taught.[159] They had three children.

When the Nazis came to power, Homberger and his family migrated to the United States in 1933. He established a private practice in child psychoanalysis in Boston while holding academic positions at the Harvard Medical School and Yale School of Medicine.[160] It was while he taught at the Harvard Medical School that "he met psychologists like Henry Murray and Kurt Lewin, and anthropologists like Ruth Benedict, Margaret Mead and Gregory Bateson. I think it can be safely said that these anthropologists had nearly as great an effect on Erikson as Sigmund and Anna Freud!"[161] In 1939, Erik Homberger became a citizen of the United States of America and changed his name to Erik Homberger Erikson.[162]

In 1950, Erik Erikson wrote "Childhood and Society, which contained summaries of his studies among the native Americans, analyses of Maxim Gorky and Adolph Hitler, a discussion of the 'American personality,' and the basic outline of his version of Freudian theory. These themes — the influence of culture on personality and the analysis of historical figures — were repeated in other works, one of which, Gandhi's Truth, won him the Pulitzer Prize and the national Book Award."[163]

Other major publications of Erik Erikson are *Young Man Luther* (1958), *Insight and Responsibility* (1964), *Identity and Crisis* (1968), *Dimensions of A New Identity* (1974), *Life History and the Historical Moment* (1975), *Dialogue with Erik Erikson*, Richard I. Evans (Ed.), Jason Aronson (1996), and with his wife, Joan, as co-author, *The Life Cycle Completed* (1987). According to Arlene F. Harder, MA, MFT, in her article, "The Developmental Stages of Erik Erikson," Erikson's basic philosophy on psychological development is that:

> Our personality traits come in opposites. We think of ourselves as optimistic or pessimistic, independent or dependent, emotional or unemotional, adventurous or cautious, leader or follower, aggressive or passive. Many of these are inborn temperament traits, but other characteristics, such as feeling either competent or inferior, appear to be learned, based on the challenges and support we receive in growing up.

> ...Although he was influenced by Freud, he believed that the ego exists from birth and that behavior is not totally defensive. Based in part on his study of Sioux Indians on a reservation, Erikson became aware of the massive influence of culture on behavior and placed more emphasis on the external world, such as depressions and wars. He felt the course of development is determined by the interaction of the body (genetic biological programming), mind (psychological), **and** cultural (ethos) influences.[164]

Erik Erikson died on 12th May 1994 in Harwick, Massachusetts. It can be said that his life was long enough to bear testimony to all the stages of psychosocial development which he is still well-known for even to this day.

B. CONCEPTS OF PSYCHOLOGY

Erik Erikson's focus was on the psychosocial development of human beings. He saw life as consisting of eight stages from birth to death. The eight stages are: infant (birth to 1 year), toddler (2 to 3 years), preschooler (3 to 6 years), school-age (6 to 12 years), adolescence (12 to 18 years), young adult (18 to 30 years), middle adult (late 20's to 50's), and old adult (50's and beyond). The ages, especially in the adult years, can vary.

In the identification of these eight stages by Erikson, Arlene F. Harder observes:

> Erikson's basic philosophy might be said to rest on two major themes: (1) the world gets bigger as we go along and (2) failure is cumulative. While the first point is fairly obvious, we might take exception to the last. True, in many cases an individual who has to deal with horrendous circumstances as a child may be unable to negotiate later stages as easily as someone who didn't have as many challenges early on. For example, we know that orphans who weren't held or stroked as infants have an extremely hard time connecting with others when they become adults and have even died from lack of human contact.
>
> However, there's always the chance that somewhere along the way the strength of the human spirit can be ignited and deficits overcome...[165]

Erikson's intent was for us to identify where our strengths are and to work towards strengthening those areas in our lives that could be improved. It is a challenge rather than an indictment.

1. Infant (Birth to 1 year)
    Basic Trust versus Basic Mistrust

    This stage is also referred to by Erik Erikson as the

"oral" stage and extends over the twelve to eighteen months of a child's life.[166] The task is for the infant to develop greater sense of trust than mistrust. Erikson points out that, "What we here call 'trust' coincides with what Therese Benedek has called 'confidence'."[167] Dr. C. George Boeree explains that:

> If mom and dad can give the newborn a degree of familiarity, consistency, and continuity, then the child will develop the feeling that the world – especially the social world – is a safe place to be, that people are reliable and loving. Through the parents' responses, the child also learns to trust his or her own body and the biological urges that go with it.
>
> If the parents are unreliable and inadequate, if they reject the infant or harm it, if other interests cause both parents to turn away from the infant's needs to satisfy their own instead, then the infant will develop mistrust. He or she will be apprehensive and suspicious around people.[168]

However, if a child is raised to be too trusting, that can be harmful in later years. The parents may not do the child any harm, but there are other people in the larger world who have evil intents. This probably accounts for many of the kidnappings and sexual abuse of children that are so frequent in our time. On the other hand, should children develop too much mistrust, "They will develop the **malignant tendency** of **withdrawal**, characterized by depression, paranoia, and possibly psychosis."[169]

When a proper balance is established, the children develop a sense of faith and hope. If needs are not satisfied immediately, they develop the sense of waiting. They know that mom or dad will satisfy their need as soon as is possible. In later life, they are able to face disappointments and failures. If things do not work out for good now, they will eventually.[170] Note that the most significant relationship at this stage is with the mother.

2. Toddler (2 to 3 years)
   Autonomy versus Shame and Doubt

This stage is also referred to by Erikson as the anal-muscular stage and extends from about eighteen months to three years. He asserts, "The over-all significance of this stage lies in the maturation of the muscular system...Psychoanalysis has enriched our vocabulary with the word 'anality' to designate the particular pleasurableness and willfulness which often attach to the eliminative organs at this stage."[171] The task for the child is to acquire a degree of autonomy and minimize shame and doubt. Dr. Boeree says that,

> If mom and dad (and the other care-takers that often come into the picture at this point) permit the child, now a toddler, to explore and manipulate his or her environment, the child will develop a sense of autonomy or independence. The parents should not discourage the child, but neither should they push. A balance is required. People often advise new parents to be "firm but tolerant" at this stage, and the advice is good. This way, the child will develop both self-control and self-esteem.
>
> On the other hand, it is rather easy for the child to develop instead a sense of shame and doubt. If the parents come down hard on any attempt to explore and be independent, the child will soon give up with the assumption that [they] cannot and should not act on their own. We should keep in mind that even something as innocent as laughing at the toddler's efforts

can lead the child to feel deeply ashamed, and to doubt his or her abilities.[172]

Note that shame and doubt can also result by giving the child too much freedom and no sense of limits. The child might develop the belief that he or she is not good enough. Parents' lack of patience can also produce shame and doubt. If we do not give a child enough time to do something, then the child begins to feel inadequate. If there is little shame or doubt, impulsiveness might result. On the other hand, if there is too much shame and doubt, compulsiveness can emerge.[173] Furthermore, we are to bear in mind that "To develop autonomy, a firmly developed and a convincingly continued stage of early trust is necessary."[174]

If there is a proper balance between autonomy and shame and doubt, the child develops will-power and determination.

3. Pre-schooler (3 to 6 years)
    Initiative versus Guilt

Erikson also calls this stage the genital-locomotor stage and extends from three to six years. He says that at this stage, "a focused interest may now develop in the genitalia of both sexes," and there is "increased locomoter mastery."[175] The task for the child is to learn initiative while keeping a sense of guilt at a minimum.

According to Dr. Boeree:

> Initiative means a positive response to the world's challenges, taking on responsibilities, learning new skills, feeling purposeful. Parents can encourage initiative by encouraging children to try out their ideas. We should accept and encourage fantasy and curiosity and imagination. This is a time for play, not for

formal education. The child is now capable, as never before, of imagining a future situation, one that isn't a reality now. Initiative is the attempt to make that non-reality a reality.

But if children can imagine the future, if they can plan, then they can be responsible as well, and guilty…[176]

Should there be too much initiative, the child can become ruthless. What is important to the child is having his or her own way without any consideration for others. Too much guilt, on the other hand, results in inhibition. The inhibited child refrains from trying anything to avoid guilt from making mistakes. Of course, the aim is to have a balance between initiative and guilt, to develop a sense of purpose and courage.[177]

4. School-age (6 to 12 years)
    Industry versus Inferiority

Erikson says this is the latency stage and extends from six to twelve years. The task is to develop a sense of industry and to avoid a sense of inadequacy or inferiority. Erikson agrees that when children "become dissatisfied and disgruntled without a sense of being useful, without a sense of being able to make things and make them well and even perfectly: this is what I call the *sense of industry*."[178] He cautions, "The danger at this stage is the development of a sense of *inadequacy and inferiority*."[179] We have the capacity to learn, create and acquire new skills and knowledge and this happens when there is a sense of industry. Dr. Boeree asserts:

There is a much broader social sphere at work now: The parents and other family members are joined by teachers and peers and other members of the commu-

nity at large. They all contribute: Parents must encourage, teachers must care, peers must accept. Children must learn that there is a pleasure not only in
conceiving a plan, but in carrying it out. They must
learn the feeling of success, whether it is in school or
on the playground, academic or social.

A good way to tell the difference between a child in
the third stage and one in the fourth stage is to look at
the way they play games. Four-year-olds may love
games, but they will have only a vague understanding
of the rules, may change them several times during
the course of the game, and be very unlikely to actually finish the game, unless it is by throwing the pieces
at their opponents. A seven-year-old, on the other
hand, is dedicated to the rules, considers them pretty
much sacred, and is more likely to get upset if the
game is not allowed to come to its required conclusion.[180]

A child who has too much industry ends up being a
narrow virtuosity or a prodigy with narrow interests. Such a
child usually does not possess any social ills. On the other
hand, a child with inferiority complexes usually suffers from
inertia. The child fails at something but never tries again.
The aim is to have a good balance between industry and inferiority and this is what is called competency.[181]

5. Adolescence (12 to 18 years)
    Identity versus Identity Diffusion

This stage extends from twelve to eighteen years. The
task during adolescence is to find our own identity and avoid
identity diffusion or role confusion. According to Erik
Erikson, at this stage of psychosocial development, "The in-

tegration now taking place in the form of the ego identity is more than the sum of the childhood identifications. It is the inner capital accrued from all those experiences of each successive stage, when meaningful identification led to a successful alignment of the individual's *basic drives* with his *endowment* and his *opportunities*."[182] The aim is to discover our individual uniqueness, to separate self from family of origin and assert self as members of the general society. Dr. C. George Boeree states,

> Ego identity means knowing who you are and how you fit into the rest of society. It requires that you take all you've learned about life and yourself and mold it into a unified self-image, one that your community finds meaningful.

> There are a number of things that makes things easier: First, we should have a mainstream adult culture that is worthy of the adolescent's respect, one with good adult role models and open lines of communication.

> Further, society should provide clear **rites of passage**, certain accomplishments and rituals that help to distinguish the adult from the child...[183]

Without good adult role models and open lines of communication and appropriate rites of passage, role confusion results. The adolescent in this case suffers from identity crisis and is confused over his or her place in the world or society at large.[184]

When there is too much of a sense of identity, there is little or no tolerance for others. This is fanaticism. Lack of a sense of identity, on the other hand, leads to repudiation of self, association with fringe groups in society, and engagement in self-destructive behavior, such as drug and alcohol abuse. The result of having a healthy sense of identity is fidelity and loyalty.

6. Young Adult (18 to 30 years)
    Intimacy and Distantiation versus Self-Absorption

This stage extends from eighteen to around thirty years. The task is to achieve intimacy instead of self-absorption or isolation. Erikson states, "When childhood and youth come to an end, life, so the saying goes, begins: by which we mean work or study for a specified career, sociability with the other sex, and in time, marriage and a family of one's own. But it is only after a reasonable sense of identity has been established that real *intimacy* with the other sex (or, for that matter, with any other person or even with oneself) is possible."[185] Dr. Boeree defines intimacy in this way:

> Intimacy is the ability to be close to others, as a lover, a friend, and as a participant in society. Because you have a clear sense of who you are, you no longer need to fear "losing" yourself, as many adolescents do. The "fear of commitment" some people seem to exhibit as an example of immaturity in this stage. This fear isn't always so obvious. Many people today are always putting off the progress of their relationships: I'll get married (or have a family, or get involved in important social issues) as soon as I finish school, as soon as I have a job, as soon as I have a house, as soon as...[186]

Dr. Boeree opines, "The emphasis on careers, the isolation of urban living, the splitting apart of relationships because of our need for mobility, and the general impersonal nature of modern life prevent people from naturally developing their intimate relationships."[187]

Too much intimacy can lead to promiscuity, that is, "the tendency to become intimate too freely, too easily, and without any depth to your intimacy."[188] On the other hand, too little or no intimacy leads to exclusion, "the tendency to isolate oneself from love, friendship, and community, and to develop a certain hatefulness in compensation for one's loneliness."[189] When intimacy exists, then the virtue of love prevails.

7. Middle Adult (30 to 60 years)
    Generativity versus Stagnation

According to Erik Erikson, this stage extends from thirty to about sixty years. The task is to develop and maintain a balance between generativity and stagnation. For Erikson, "Generativity is primarily the interest in establishing and guiding the next generation, although there are people who, from misfortune or because of special and genuine gifts in other directions, do not apply this drive to offspring but to other forms of altruistic concern and of creativity, which may absorb their kind of parental responsibility."[190] Dr. Boeree explains further,

> Generativity is an extension of love into the future. It is concern for the next generation and all future generations. As such, it is considerably less "selfish" than the intimacy of the previous stage: Intimacy, the love between lovers or friends, is a love between equals, and it is necessarily reciprocal. Oh, of course we love each other unselfishly, but the reality is such that, if the love is not returned, we don't consider it a true love. With generativity, that implicit expectation of reciprocity isn't there, at least not as strongly. Few parents expect a "return on their investment" from their children. If they do, we don't think of them as

very good parents![191]

   Note, however, that there are ways other than having children by which people can be generative. Erikson believes that "teaching, writing, invention, the arts and sciences, social activism, and generally contributing to the welfare of future generations to be generativity as well..."[192] The absence of generativity is stagnation, that is, concern is only for the self and no one else. When there is too much generativity, there is overextension, lack of care for oneself. Lack of generativity results in rejectivity or a withdrawal into oneself.[193] When there is a balance between generativity and stagnation, the virtue is care.

8.   Old Adult (60 years to Death)
     Integrity versus Despair and Disgust

   This stage extends from sixty years until the time of death. The task is to increase integrity while minimizing despair at the same time. Erik Erikson explains what he means by integrity when he writes, "Only he who in some way has taken care of things and people and has adapted himself to the triumphs and disappointments of being, by necessity, the originator of others and the generator of things and ideas— only he may gradually grow the fruit of the seven stages. I know no better word for it than *integrity*."[194] On the other hand, "Despair expresses the feeling that the time is short, too short for the attempt to start another life and to try out alternate roads to integrity."[195] In describing this stage, Dr. C. George Boeree explains, thus:

      First comes a detachment from society, from a sense of usefulness, for most people in our culture. Some retire from jobs they've held for years; others find their duties as parents coming to a close; most find that their input is no longer requested or required.

Then there is a sense of biological uselessness, as the body no longer does everything it used to. Women go through a sometimes dramatic menopause; Men often find they can no longer "rise to the occasion." Then there are the illnesses of old age, such as arthritis, diabetes, heart problems, concerns about breast and ovarian and prostate cancers. Then come fears about things that one was never afraid of before – the flu, for example, or just falling down.

Along with the illnesses come concerns of death. Friends die. Relatives die. One's spouse dies. It is, of course, certain that you, too, will have your turn. Faced with all this, it might seem like everyone would feel despair.[196]

Dr. Boeree defines integrity as "coming to terms with your life, and thereby coming to terms with the end of life."[197] Some people also become absorbed with their past. If there have been mistakes in the past, in this stage we have to forgive ourselves. In the absence of all this, one can easily sink into despair.

When integrity does not deal honestly with the problems of old age, presumption results. Instead of having a positive outlook, when integrity faces up to the problems of old age, disdain could emerge and this is characterized by a hatred of life.

Erik Erikson's eight stages of psychosocial development has value for us in that it provides us with a framework for understanding and evaluating some aspects of our lives which can result in change for a fuller life.

C. THE MEDIATOR AND PSYCHOLOGICAL CONCEPTS

Erik Erikson's focus was on psychosocial development of human beings which extends from birth to death. He divides up the time in between into eight stages. This is important to mediation because a mediator, like any other human being, develops qualities during these eight stages which they bring into the mediation room.

It is in the first stage, birth to one year, that trust is developed. Of course the opposite of trust is lack of trust or mistrust. The mediator has to have trust in the process as well as in the disputants. Order runs through the process. It is a step by step procedure which hopefully leads to reconciliation and an agreement between parties in dispute. The process is not perfect, but it is the best we have. The disputants are the ones who know what they want in order to reach an agreement. But they have had no formal training in the process. The mediator has. Therefore, the mediator is entrusted with the process to encourage, enable and empower the disputants to bring out that which is already in them. Consequently, the experienced mediator knows that trust is required, trust in the process and trust in the disputants.

Trust is a prerequisite in facilitative mediation, and even more so in transformative mediation. Transformative mediation demands a great deal of trust in the parties in dispute, for it focuses on the human element and the potential it brings into the mediation room. The mediator must have a great capacity to trust in this respect.

The presence of trust enables the mediator to be optimistic and hopeful that the two parties will work towards the best solution that they are capable of reaching. Trust also fosters patience, a sense of waiting, and letting the process emerge naturally instead of forcing it. It is true that the mediator has the right to say to the disputants that they need to move forward, mindful that this is different from merely hurrying the process prematurely. Of course, while mediators always like to conclude a case with an agreement, only eighty-five percent of all cases do, according to statistics from Community Mediation Services, Jamaica, New York, where I serve as a volunteer mediator. The capacity to trust, according to Erikson, will enable mediators to accept disappointments and failures whenever they do occur.

In the second stage, two to three years old, the issues are autonomy vs. shame and doubt. The development of autonomy is an important factor when it comes to controlling the process of mediation by the mediator. The lack of autonomy leads to shame and doubt. These, in turn, result in impulsiveness and compulsiveness depending on the extent of the shame and doubt that are present. The mediator can confuse the disputants if uncontrollable impulsiveness or compulsiveness begin to surface within that mediator.

Stage three, three to six years old, has to do with issues of initiative vs. guilt. A mediator must be able to take initiatives, for this is part of assuming and maintaining control of the process. The mediator, however, must be able to differentiate between taking the initiative and being over-zealous which can lead to depriving disputants from exercising their initiative. The success of mediation depends on the ability of the disputants to show some initiative in the mediation process, and a mediator must recognize and look for opportunities to encourage it.

Stage four, six to twelve years old, focuses on the issues of industry vs. inferiority. In mediation, the issue to be concerned over is that of inferiority. This is parallel to Carl Jung's concept of the inferiority complex. As is true in the case of an inferiority complex, a sense of inadequacy or inferiority in a mediator may lead to difficulty in moving the process along, for that mediator may not be assertive enough. When both disputants are angry, a mediator has to be assertive in order to maintain control of the process. Note that for

Erikson, when the presence of inferiority is acknowledged by the mediator, it can be overcome by industry, as was mentioned earlier, by developing "the capacity to learn, create and acquire new skills and knowledge."

In the adolescence stage, stage 5 which is twelve to eighteen years old, the issues are identity vs. identity diffusion. The main issue here is having a good sense of self-identity which is also called ego identity. Ego identity has some similarities to Freud's and Jung's concepts of the ego. Earlier, Dr. C. George Boeree says that Erikson's "Ego identity means knowing who you are and how you fit into the rest of society." The ego identity is the sum total of all of a life's experiences up to the present. The broader the experiences become as life progresses, the healthier is the ego identity and the more equipped the mediator will be in dealing with disputants and co-mediators as human beings. It is crucial for teenage mediators to know this as they serve among their peers in school systems.

Stage six, eighteen to thirty years old, the issues are intimacy vs. self-absorption. Mediators maintain a professional distance in respect to disputants. Intimacy, therefore, is not encouraged so as not to create the perception of partiality. Another issue in this stage that pertains to the mediation process is that of isolation. A mediator can become ineffective if depression or low self-esteem or low self-worth accompanies the isolation.

Most mediators come from the next two stages, seven and eight. For stage seven, the age group is thirty to sixty years old and their issues are generativity vs. stagnation. Dr. Boeree states previously that Erikson believed that "teaching, writing, invention, the arts and sciences, social activism, and generally contributing to the welfare of future generations to be generativity as well..." I believe that peacemaking can be added to this list. My motivation for becoming a volunteer mediator was to bring peace in my own small way to my local community, so that it will be a better place for future generations to live in. In speaking with other volunteer mediators, I have found that basically this is their motivation too.

In stage eight, sixty years old to death, the issues are integrity vs. despair and disgust. This is the stage at which people usually retire from regular employment. It is the stage when people come to terms with their aging process and the fragility of their lives, more specifically, the end of their lives, death. At this stage, to remain active and still make a contribution to society at the same time, some people choose to become volunteer mediators. This most likely helps them to avoid despair or disgust and helps them to maintain integrity in their lives. This is a good place to be in life – a peacemaker, a mediator, regardless of mediation style.

CHAPTER VII

ABRAHAM MASLOW

A. LIFE AND TIMES

Dr. C. George Boeree in his article, "Abraham Maslow: 1908-1970," tells us that Abraham Harold Maslow was born in Brooklyn, New York, on 1 April 1908 to a poor, uneducated Jewish family who were immigrants from Russia.[198] He was the oldest of seven children and like most immigrants to the United States of America who came here with nothing but the clothes on their backs, saw education for their children as the opportunity for advancement in this country and a new life. To them, education was the great equalizer. Initially, to satisfy his parents' desire, Maslow began to study law at City College of New York. Later, he transferred to Cornell University but returned to City College not too long after.

Maslow married Bertha Goodman, his first cousin, and they had two daughters.[199] Bertha moved with her husband to Wisconsin where he attended the University of Wisconsin. It was here that "he became interested in psychology, and his school work began to improve dramatically. He spent time there working with Harry Harlow, who is famous for his experiments with baby rhesus monkeys and attachment behavior."[200] Maslow went on to earn his Bachelor of Arts, Master of Arts and Doctor of Philosophy degrees in psychology at the University of Wisconsin between 1930 and 1934. After further research, he went to teach and continue in research on human sexuality at Columbia University.

Later on, Maslow became a full-time teacher at Brooklyn College and "During this period of his life, he came into contact with the many European intellectuals that were immigrating to the US, and Brooklyn in particular, at that time – people like Adler, Fromm, Horney, as well as several Gestalt and Freudian psychologists."[201]

But Abraham Maslow's teaching career did not end at Brooklyn College. In 1951, he "served as the chair of the psychology department at Brandeis for 10 years, where he met Kurt Goldstein (who introduced him to the idea of self-actualization) and began his own theoretical work. It was also here that he began his crusade for a humanistic psychology – something ultimately much more important to him than his own theorizing."[202]

During Maslow's time, there were two other "main branches of psychology, Freudianism, based on the teachings of Sigmund Freud, and Behaviorism based on the works of B. F. Skinner and John Watson."[203] Maslow noticed that there were some shortcomings in these two branches of psychology. Sigmund Freud had focused only on neurotic and psychotic people in his work. Even though Skinner and Watson had worked with ordinary people, "Maslow believed they reflected only what was present, and not the potential to be realized in individuals…This soon became the premise behind the school of humanistic psychology as we know it today, and included the views that a person's psyche must be viewed through a holistic approach, in order to fully understand how to affect it…"[204]

Abraham Maslow wrote several books, but the best known are *Toward A Psychology of Being* (1968), *Motivation and Personality* (1970), and *The Further Reaches of Human Nature* (1971). His most popular book is *Toward A Psychology of Being* which brought him recognition as a significant psychologist. Betty Dintelman points out that:

> It is in this work that he outlined the hierarchy of needs which would be the defining element of his career.

The five tiered pyramid consisted of physiological needs, safety needs, social needs, esteem needs, and self-actualization needs...Maslow arrived at this pinnacle in his career by using unique research methods in defining the hierarchy. By studying the characteristics of human beings who were self-actualized, ("growing tips" he called them), he was able to define a set of characteristics which he felt each of them possessed, and then classify those characteristics to outline the needs met...Among his subjects were Abraham Lincoln, Albert Einstein, Eleanor Roosevelt, Harriet Tubman, Ralph Waldo Emerson, Thomas Jefferson, Henry Wadsworth Longfellow, and numerous others. His hierarchy would increase in popularity with the publications of McGregor, a fellow psychologist of the time...His studies and resulting theories would attribute to him the title of Father of Humanistic Psychology, and provide a tool for the basic foundations of the study of human motivation and needs...[205]

The psychologist whom Betty Dintelman referred to as "McGregor" is Douglas McGregor whose main interest was managerial psychology. Maslow's theory on the hierarchy of needs had a great impact on McGregor who made it the foundation for his Theory X and Theory Y concepts. "Douglas McGregor wrote *The Human Side of Enterprise* in 1960. He quickly became known as the father of Theory X and Theory Y—theories of managerial leadership that portrayed managers as authoritarian (Theory X) or as collaborative and trustful of people (Theory Y). In outlining Theory Y, McGregor clearly subscribed to Maslow's view of human nature. In fact, McGregor used much of Maslow's research on the hierarchy of motivation to develop his assumptions of the Theory Y manager."[206]

Abraham Maslow suffered from ill-health in his latter years and eventually died of a heart attack on the 8th June, 1970 in Menlo Park, California. He was sixty-two years old when he died.[207]

B. CONCEPTS OF PSYCHOLOGY

Abraham Maslow is regarded as the Father of humanistic psychology, out of which, the theory of the hierarchy of needs emerged. Before examining the hierarchy of needs, it is important that we first understand the world-view of the humanist. The article, "Maslow's Hierarchy of Needs," which is based on the book, *Psychology – The Search for Understanding*, written by Janet A. Simons, Donald B. Irwin and Beverly A Drinnien, asserts,

> Humanists do not believe that human beings are pushed and pulled by mechanical forces, either of stimuli and reinforcements (behaviorism) or of unconscious instinctual impulses (psychoanalysis). Humanists focus upon potentials. They believe that humans strive for an upper level of capabilities. Humans seek the frontiers of creativity, the highest reaches of consciousness and wisdom. This has been labeled "fully functioning person", "healthy personality", or as Maslow calls this level, "self-actualizing person."[208]

Of course, the environment is an important factor in the progression toward self-actualization. If the environment does not offer the opportunities and support in order for someone to become self-actualized, it will not happen.

Another important point to bear in mind about Maslow's world-view is that,

He felt that people are basically trustworthy, self-pro-
tecting, and self-governing. Humans tend toward
growth and love. Although there is a continuous cycle
of human wars, murder, deceit, etc., he believed that
violence is not what human nature is meant to be like.
Violence and other evils occur when human needs are
thwarted. In other words, people who are deprived of
lower needs such as safety may defend themselves by
violent means. He did not believe that humans are
violent because they enjoy violence. Or that they lie,
cheat, and steal because they enjoy doing it.[209]

Anyway, "Maslow's defining work was perhaps his
development of the hierarchy of needs. Maslow believed that
human beings aspired to become self-actualizing. He viewed
human potential as vastly underestimated and an unexplained
territory."[210] Dr. C. George Boeree says that Maslow arrived
at his theory on the hierarchy of needs from his observation
of the behavior of the baby rhesus monkeys that he worked
with earlier in his career.[211] It was then that he noticed that
some needs were more significant than others. "For example,
if you are hungry and thirsty, you will tend to try to take care
of the thirst first. After all, you can do without food for weeks,
but you can only do without water for a couple of days!"[212]
Based on his observations, Maslow developed his theory on
the hierarchy of needs. The five needs that he identified are
"the physiological needs, the needs for safety and security,
the needs for love and belonging, the needs for esteem, and
the need to actualize the self, in that order."[213]
Brief descriptions of each set of needs are as follows:

1. Physiological Needs

Physiological needs are biological or survival needs
which are required to sustain life. They include air, water,

drink, sleep, warmth, shelter, sex, protein, salt, sugar, miner-
als, vitamins, elimination of body waste, to avoidance of pain,
etc. Robert J Sternberg observes, "Even in affluent countries
many people live in poverty and struggle daily to meet this
most basic level of needs."[214]   When these needs are unmet,
we may experience pain, sickness, anxiety, discomfort, anger, etc.

2. Safety and Security Needs

Safety and security needs are psychological needs which
have to do with shelter and protection.[215] These "are second-
ary to the absolute necessities; when the physiological needs
are met, then a second layer of needs becomes prominent."[216]
The safety and security needs include protection from the elements, safe neighborhood, job security, financial security,
health insurance, structure, protection, order, stability, law,
limits, home, family, etc. When a person is attacked or when
a neighborhood is unsafe, there is no security or safety. When
these needs are unmet, the result is fear and anxiety, etc.

3. Love and Belonging Needs

Love and belonging needs are social needs, that is, "to
feel that other people love and care about us and to be a part
of a meaningful group, such as a family. The bond between
children and their parents shows how important this need
is."[217] They include family, relationships, friendship, affec-
tion, group membership, membership in a work team, etc.
When these needs are unmet, the result is loneliness and associated anxiety.

4. Self-Esteem Needs

Self-esteem needs have to do with feeling worthwhile.[218] They are divided into two groups. One group has to do with our interaction with others, for example, status prestige, appreciation, recognition, respect from others, attention, fame, glory, dominance, reputation, etc. The second group of needs is subjective, namely, self-esteem, self-worth, self-respect, achievement, mastery, etc. When these needs are not satisfied, the result is low self-esteem, inferiority complex, helplessness, weakness, worthlessness, etc.

5. Self-Actualization Needs

Self-actualization needs are the needs to become all that one has the potential or is capable of becoming. It is "a continuing desire to 'be all that you can be'."[219] It is becoming what one was born to be. It is the need to feel fulfilled, to have a sense of peace, happiness and harmony in one's life. It is the need to experience meaning, truth, wisdom, knowledge, and a feeling of being at oneness with God. Note, however, that while "a self-actualizing person is someone who is really quite extraordinary, he or she can nonetheless give the impression of being entirely conventional. A self-actualizing person does not *need* to prove anything by being deliberately eccentric or unconventional."[220]

In his article, "maslow's hierarchy of needs," Alan Chapman points out that:

Maslow's Hierarchy of Needs states that we must satisfy each need in turn, starting with the first, which deals with the most obvious needs for survival itself.

Only when the lower order needs of physical and emotional well-being are satisfied are we concerned with the higher order needs of influence and personal development.

Conversely, if the things that satisfy our lower order needs are swept away, we are no longer concerned about the maintenance of our higher order needs.[221]

Chapman tells us further, "You can't motivate someone to achieve their sales target (level 4) when they're having problems with their marriage (level 3). You can't expect someone to work as a team member (level 3) when they're having their house re-possessed (level 2)."[222] However, the aim in life should be to move up to higher levels than where we currently are and this eventually results in self-actualization.

Robert J Sternberg describes self-actualized people in this way:

Self-actualized people are free of mental illness and have reached the top of the hierarchy of needs. They have experienced love and have a full sense of their self-worth and value. They accept both themselves and others unconditionally and accept what the world brings to them. They have a keen perception of reality and can discern genuineness in others, shunning phoniness in themselves. They are neutral and ethical in their dealings with others. As they face the events in their lives, they are problem-centered, seeing problems for what they are, rather than seeing all problems in relation to themselves and their own needs. They are able to be alone without constantly feeling lonely, and they have the ability to map out their own paths. They have constructed their own system of beliefs and values and do not need others to agree with them in order to hold true to what they stand for. They appreciate and enjoy life and live it to its fullest.[223]

Of course, the question arises as to if a person can really achieve full self-actualization and, if so, can that person then lose it later on. I believe that self-actualization can be achieved by someone, but that person does not remain in that self-actualized state for the rest of his or her life because of the changing nature of this world and this life. One has to work constantly to regain the self-actualized state. It is an ongoing process.

C. THE MEDIATOR AND PSYCHOLOGICAL CONCEPTS

In their book, *Getting to Yes: Negotiating Agreement Without Giving In*, Roger Fisher, William Ury and Bruce Patton advise that in any effort in conflict resolution, the focus should not be on positions of the parties involved because it can be difficult to make people change them. They assert, "The more you clarify your position and defend it against attack, the more committed you become to it."[224] Instead, they suggest that the focus should be on interests or needs.[225] Mediators as peacemakers, therefore, have to be concerned with needs. In order to reduce the tension in the mediation room as much as possible, the mediator must focus on the needs of all the parties present. To this end, Abraham Maslow's theory on the hierarchy of needs would prove to be extremely helpful in identifying needs as they affect mediation.

First of all, as mediators we have to ask ourselves, "What is my need as a mediator?" "Why am I sitting in this mediation room with two parties in dispute who are complete strangers to me?" I became a volunteer mediator because I wanted to do something to help bring peace into the lives of people in conflict situations in my local community. This is my small contribution to help make the community in which I live a better place to live in. Additionally, it is my belief is that I did this because of self-actualization needs, the fifth or highest level of needs according to Maslow. I had a need to be fulfilled and have a sense of peace, happiness and harmony in my life. The way I sought to satisfy this need was through mediation. There are volunteer mediators with whom I serve and they too became mediators to satisfy self-actualization needs.

Some volunteers are retired and became mediators because they wanted to experience a sense of accomplishment, a sense of achievement. The need they were seeking to fulfill is that of self-esteem, the fourth level of needs. There are also some retired people who became volunteer mediators in order to belong to a group. They became a part of a meaningful group of mediators which replaced the group of people they were part of before they retired from regular employment. This is a belonging need, the third level in Maslow's hierarchy of needs. I do not think that people become volunteer mediators to satisfy a physiological need, the first or lowest level in the hierarchy of needs, or to fulfill a safety or security need, the second level of needs.

We looked at the personal needs of mediators. Now, we will look at the needs of disputants. Each disputant comes to mediation with needs. All parties in a dispute come to mediation with a need to be treated fairly and justly, a self-esteem need. This is why a mediator must be, as well as appear to be, impartial and neutral.

From my experience in landlord/tenant cases, tenants usually have complaints which have to do with physiological needs or safety and security needs. When the needs are physiological, the issues are usually about lack of water, lack of heat or lack of electricity. Usually, the tenant's claim is that the landlord is deliberately withholding the water or heat or electricity or there is a breakdown of equipment or infrastructure and the landlord is doing nothing to get it fixed. In regards to safety and security needs, some of the things tenants complain about are leaking roofs and broken windows, and in the case of apartments or multiple family buildings, broken locks on the main front door.

On the other hand, the common complaint from landlords has to do with no payment or willful withholding of rent by tenants. This is a level two need, a security need. The landlord's concern is with his financial security. Will he be able to pay the mortgage, utility bills and building maintenance costs if the tenant continues not to pay the rent?

In parent/teen mediation, some issues surround love and belonging needs. Parents and children need to be loved by each other, to know that that special bond exists between them. When the bond of love is broken, parents and children feel alienated from each other and the vacuum within them is usually filled with anger and resentment. Another set of needs that have an impact on parent/teen mediation as well as peer mediation in schools is that of self-esteem needs. Many problems that lead to these two forms of mediation involve young people whose self-esteem needs are unmet. The result, as was pointed out earlier, is "low self-esteem, inferiority complex, helplessness, weakness, worthlessness, etc." This accounts for a great deal of anger, lack of interest in studies at school, substance abuse, promiscuous behavior and truancy among our young people. Note that Carl Jung and Erik Erikson also referred to feelings of inferiority and the devastating toll it takes on the ego.

In Chapter II, the mediation place was explored. Mediators have the responsibility to ensure that physiological needs are provided for everyone. They must check to see that there is adequate lighting, adequate heating or cooling, adequate ventilation, adequate-size room for the number of disputants, easily accessible restroom facilities, etc. Safety and security needs must also be addressed through the provision of adequate security within or surrounding the office building. At Community Mediation Services where I serve as a mediator, it is not unusual for a security person to knock on the door if there is excessive shouting in a room where a mediation case is in progress to find out if everything is all right.

Finally, there is another need, a self-esteem need, which mediators and parties in a dispute usually expect to be met in the mediation room. This need is "to be respected by others." Occasionally, there are times when a disputant may forget that respect is mutual, that you cannot only expect to receive respect but you have to be willing to give it as well. This is why mediators issue a reminder about this in their opening statements. Their task is to point out to the disputants that they are to respect each other by not shouting at each other, not calling each other names, and not interrupting when the other person is speaking. Mediators do this to satisfy this basic need of the disputants as human beings.

Of course, mediators also have the need to be respected as human beings. They need respect too for another reason - to control the process. This is the reason why mediators will not pursue a case if any of the disputants is under the influence of alcohol or drugs or is mentally unstable.

Mediators have to be concerned with satisfying needs in mediation. They protect the process, maintain control, avoid violence, and assure the safety and mutual respect for all parties in the mediation room.

CHAPTER VIII

CONCLUSION

In our journey through this study, we became familiar with what mediation is from an examination of some definitions of mediation. Next, we looked at the major elements of mediation, that is, the place of the mediation, the person of the mediator, and the mediation process. In other words, we found out what mediation is, where it is done, who does it, and how it is done. The focus then shifted to the various styles or approaches that the mediators use in performing their functions, namely, facilitative mediation, transformative mediation, evaluative mediation and restorative justice mediation.

After exploring the world of mediation for a while to acquaint ourselves with its major dimensions, we looked at the life and times and the major psychological concepts of Sigmund Freud, Carl Gustav Jung, Erik Homberger Erikson and Abraham Maslow. For each one, we saw how the author's psychological concepts play out in the lives of mediators as human beings, the effect they have on their tasks and responsibilities, and in some way, on how they perform them, that is, their mediation style.

We saw that the psychological concepts of Freud, Jung, Erikson and Maslow do have a profound influence on mediators and on their mediation styles, not because they are different from people in general, but, on the contrary, simply because they are human beings like anyone else. The concepts of the four authors describe people as individuals and explain to some extent that in the process of growing up as children and young people and in the process of getting older as adults, that life's circumstances and the influence that people exercise in our lives have a great deal to do with who we are today. This same human element is what we find in the mediation room as the mediator.

In this study, we witnessed how the psychological entities, described in the concepts of the authors, play out in this particular human activity of mediation, of peacemaking in conflict situations involving two parties. We have seen that they do affect the behavior of the mediator, the way a mediator relate to disputants and co-mediators, the communication style of the mediator, and the style with which a mediator is most comfortable, namely, facilitative mediation, transformative mediation, evaluative mediation or restorative justice mediation. In other words, we saw how the psychological elements interplay with each other in the person of the mediator as human being.

It is my hope that by becoming aware of the presence of the psychological elements within us and the way they influence who we are, what we do, why we do them and how we do them, that the work of mediation will become more significant and exciting for us and that we, as mediators, will become more effective because of this. My wish is that mediators will find this paper useful, too, regardless of whether they are in the community or ecclesial setting, for the approach in each is basically the same.

Finally, this study can serve as a bridge between mediation and the cognate fields of psychology, sociology, social work, pastoral counseling and pastoral psychology. Pastoral counselors, psychotherapists and psychologists, for instance, will see that there are fundamentals in their respective fields which are similar to those of mediation. This paper will help to facilitate the inclusion of mediation in their professional study.

ENDNOTES

[1] Sharon C. Leviton and James L. Greenstone, *Elements of Mediation* (Pacific Grove, California: Brooks/Cole Publishing Company, 1997), 1.

[2] Ibid.

[3] Jennifer Beer with Eileen Stief, *The Mediator's Handbook* (Canada: New Society Publishers, 1997), 3.

[4] Ibid.

[5] This information is found on the outside back cover.

[6] Ibid.

[7] Selma Myers and Barbara Filner, "Mediation Concepts," *Conflict Resolution Across Cultures: From Talking It Out to Third Party Mediation*: 1; available from http://www.diversityresources.com/rc21d/mediation.html; Internet; accessed 2 January 2004.

[8] "Mediation": 1; available from http://www.spea.indiana.edu/lbingham/v547/Mediation%20Introduction.htm; Internet; accessed 20 September 2004.

[9] Rob Scott, "The NVMS Approach to Mediation," *Northern Virginia Mediation Service Resolutionary* 1996-2003: 1; available from http://www.gmu.edu/departments/nvms/mediate.htm; Internet; accessed 20 September 2004.

[10] Robert A Baruch Bush and Joseph P. Folger, *The Promise of Mediation: The Transformative Approach to Conflict*, Revised Edition (San Francisco, CA: Jossey-Bass, 2005), 8.

[11] Myers and Filner, "Mediation Concepts," 3.

[12] Beer with Stief, *The Mediator's Handbook*, 16.

[13] Leviton and Greenstone, *Elements of Mediation*, 17.

[14] Ibid.

[15] Ibid.

[16] Ibid., 17-18.

[17] Beer with Stief, *The Mediator's Handbook*, 28.

[18] Ibid.

[19] Leviton and Greenstone, *Elements of Mediation*, 18.

[20] Ibid., 10.

[21] Ibid., 11.

[22] Beer with Stief, *The Mediator's Handbook*, 23.

[23] Leviton and Greenstone, *Elements of Mediation*, 11.

[24] Rob Scott, "The NVMS Approach to Mediation," 2.

[25] Leviton and Greenstone, *Elements of Mediation*, 11.

[26] Ibid., 11-16.

[27] Beer with Stief, *The Mediator's Handbook*, 4-5.

[28] Myers and Filner, "Mediation Concepts," 3.

[29] Leviton and Greenstone, *Elements of Mediation*, 22-30.

[30] Ibid., 31-37.

[31] Ibid., 31.

[32] Beer with Stief, *The Mediator's Handbook*, 4.

[33] Myers and Filner, "Mediation Concepts," 3.

[34] Ibid.

[35] Leviton and Greenstone, *Elements of Mediation*, 22.

[36] Ibid., 22-23.

[37] Ibid., 24.

[38] Ibid., 25.

[39] Myers and Filner, "Mediation Concepts," 3.

[40] Leviton and Greenstone, *Elements of Mediation*, 31.

[41] Ibid., 32-33.

[42] Ibid., 33.

[43] Myers and Filner, "Mediation Concepts," 3.

[44] Beer with Stief, *The Mediator's Handbook*, p. 50.

[45] Myers and Filner, "Mediation Concepts," 3.

[46] Beer with Stief, *The Mediator's Handbook*, 56.

[47] Ibid., 58.

[48] Mediation and Conflict Resolution Office, "Different Types of Mediation Styles," *The Maryland Legal Assistance Network* 1999-2004: 1; available from http://www.peoples-law.org/core/mediation/adr/_directory/mediation_approaches.htm; Internet; accessed 19 September 2004.

[49] Zena D. Zumeta, J.D., "Styles of Mediation: Facilitative, Evaluative and Transformative Mediation," 1-2; available from http://learn2mediate.com/resources/nacfm.php; Internet; accessed 4 August 2004.

[50] Ibid., 2.

[51] Mediation and Conflict Resolution Office, "Different Types of Mediation Styles," 1.

[52] Hew R. Dundas, "Mediation in England: Some Current Issues," *Oil, Gas & Energy* Volume I, issue #02, March 2003: 2; available from http://www.gasandoil.com/ogel/samples/freearticles/article_74.htm; Internet; accessed 19 September 2004.

[53] Christopher W. Moore, *The Mediation Process: Practical Strategies for Resolving Conflict*, 3rd Edition Revised, (San Francisco, California: Jossey-Bass, 2003), 55.

[54] Bush and Folger, *The Promise of Mediation*, 22-23.

[55] Mediation and Conflict Resolution Office, "Different Types of Mediation Styles," 1.

[56] Zumeta, "Styles of Mediation: Facilitative, Evaluative and Transformative Mediation," 3-4.

[57] Brad Spangler, "General Basis and Background of Transformative Mediation," *Transformative Mediation* 2003: 7; available from http://www.beyondintractability.org/m/transformative_mediation.jsp; Internet; accessed 19 September 2004.

[58] Larry Blackwell, "Transformative Mediation: A Best Fit for the Workplace," *The CEO Refresher Archives* 2004: 1; available from http://www.refresher.com/!lrbmediation.html; Internet; accessed 19 September 2004.

[59] Moore, *The Mediation Process*, 55-56.

[60] Ibid., 56.

[61] Dundas, "Mediation in England: Some Current Issues," 2.

[62] Mediation and Conflict Resolution Office, "Different Types of Mediation Styles," 1.

[63] Zumeta, J.D., "Styles of Mediation: Facilitative, Evaluative and Transformative Mediation," 2-3.

[64] Restorative Justice Online, "What Is Restorative Justice?," *Restorative Justice* 1999: 1; available from http://www.restorativejustice.org/rj3/intro_default.htm; Internet; accessed 19 September 2004.

[65] Daniel Van Ness and Karen Heetderks Strong, *Restoring Justice*, (Cincinnati, OH: Anderson Publishing Co., 1997), 31.

[66] Restorative Justice Outline, "What is Restorative Justice?," 1.

[67] Van Ness and Strong, *Restoring Justice*, 71.

[68] Ibid.

[69] Ibid.

[70] Ibid.

[71] Ibid.

[72] Ibid.

[73] Ibid., 72.

[74] Anthony Storr, *Freud*, (New York: Barnes & Noble Books, 1998), 1.

[75] Louis Breger, *Freud: Darkness in the Midst of Vision*, (New York: John Wiley & Sons, Inc., 2000), 7.

[76] Ibid., 11.

[77] Ibid., 1.

[78] Ibid., 2.

[79] Calvin S. Hall, *A Primer of Freudian Psychology* (New York, New York: Meridian, 1999), 11-12.

[80] Storr, *Freud*, 3.

[81] Ibid., 11.

[82] Dr. C. George Boeree, "Sigmund Freud: 1856 - 1939," *Personality Theories* 1997: 2; available from http://www.ship.edu/~cgboeree/freud.html; Internet; accessed 8 October 2004.

[83] Ibid.

[84] Breger, *Freud*, 305.

[85] Ibid., 362.

[86] Hall, *A Primer of Freudian Psychology*, 22.

[87] Boeree, "Sigmund Freud," 4.

[88] John H. Morgan, *Being Human: Perspectives on Meaning and Interpretation* (Bristol, IN: Quill Books, 2002), 115.

[89] Boeree, " Sigmund Freud," 4.

[90] Ibid..

[91] Sigmund Freud, *The Ego and the Id* (New York: W. W. Norton & Company, 1960), 19.

[92] Boeree, "Sigmund Freud," 4.

[93] Morgan, *Being Human*, 115-116.

[94] Boeree, "Sigmund Freud," 4.

[95] Ibid.

[96] Morgan, *Being Human*, 120.

[97] Ibid., 116.

[98] Ibid., 120.

[99] Sigmund Freud, *Inhibitions, Symptoms and Anxiety* (New York: W. W. Norton & Company, 1959), 57.

[100] Boeree, "Sigmund Freud," 5.

[101] Ibid.

[102] Ibid., 6.

[103] Hall, *A Primer of Freudian Psychology*, 86.

[104] Boeree, "Sigmund Freud," 6.

[105] Ibid.

[106] Hall, *A Primer of Freudian Psychology*, 79.

[107] Boeree, "Sigmund Freud," 7.

[108] Hall, *A Primer of Freudian Psychology*, 89.

[109] Calvin S. Hall and Vernon J. Nordby, *A Primer of Jungian Psychology* (New York, New York: Meridian, 1999), 16.

[110] Ibid., 17.

[111] Ibid., 19.

[112] Ibid., 20.

[113] Ibid.

[114] C. G. Jung, *Memories, Dreams, Reflections*, edited by Aniela Jaffe, translated by Richard and Clara Winston (New York: Vintage Books, 1965), 86.

[115] Ibid., 112.

[116] Ibid., 114.

[117] Ibid., 117.

[118] Ibid., 157-8.

[119] Hall and Nordby, *A Primer of Jungian Psychology*, 24-25.

[120] Ibid., 22.

[121] Jung, *Memories, Dreams, Reflections*, 189.

[122] Hall and Nordby, *A Primer of Jungian Psychology*, 23.

[123] Ibid., 27.

[124] Ibid.

[125] Ibid., 32.

[126] Ibid., 33.

[127] Ibid.

[128] Lee and Norma Barr, *The Leadership Equation: Leadership, Management, and the Myers-Briggs* (Austin,Texas:Eakin Press,1989), x.

[129] Hall and Nordby, *A Primer of Jungian Psychology*, 34.

[130] Ibid., 35.

[131] Lee and Norma Barr, *The Leadership Equation*, x.

[132] David Keirsey and Marilyn Bates, *Please Understand Me: Character and Temperament Types,* 4th ed. (Del Mar, California: Prometheus Nemesis Book Company, 1984), 4.

133 Ibid., 13-14.
134 Gary L. Harbaugh, *God's Gifted People: Discovering Your Personality As A Gift,* Expanded ed. (Minneapolis, Minnesota: Augsburg Fortress, 1990), 27.
135 Hall and Nordby, *A Primer of Jungian Psychology*, 35.
136 Ibid.
137 Ibid., 36.
138 Ibid.
139 Ibid., 37-38.
140 Ibid., 39.
141 Ibid.
142 Ibid., 41.
143 Ibid.
144 Ibid., 41-42.
145 Ibid., 42.
146 Ibid., 44-45.
147 Ibid., 46-47.
148 Ibid., 48.
149 Ibid., 48-49.
150 Ibid., 51.
151 Ibid., 51-52.
152 Ibid., 131.
153 Lawrence J. Friedman, *Identity's Architect: A Biography of Erik H. Erikson* (Cambridge, Massachusetts: Harvard University Press, 2000), 30.
154 Ibid. 40.
155 Ibid., 45.
156 Ibid., 57.
157 Ibid., 59.
158 Ibid.
159 Ibid., 81-82.
160 Ibid., 103.
161 Dr. C. George Boeree, "Erik Erikson: 1902 – 1994," *Personality Theories* 1997: 3; available from http://www.ship.edu/~cgboeree/erikson.html; Internet; accessed 8 October 2004.
162 Friedman, *Identity's Architect*, 144.

[163] Boeree, "Erik Erikson," 3.

[164] Arlene F. Harder, MA, MFT, "The Developmental Stages of Erik Erikson," *Learning Place Online.com* 2002: 1; available from http://www.learningplaceonline.com/stages/organize/Erikson.htm; Internet; accessed 8 October 2004.

[165] Ibid., 2.

[166] Erik H. Erikson, *Identity and the Life Cycle* (New York: W. W. Norton & Company, 1980), 59.

[167] Ibid., 63.

[168] Boeree, "Erik Erikson," 5-6.

[169] Ibid., 6.

[170] Ibid.

[171] Erikson, *Identity and the Life Cycle*, 68.

[172] Boeree, "Erik Erikson," 6.

[173] Ibid.

[174] Erikson, *Identity and the Life Cycle*, 71.

[175] Ibid., 80.

[176] Boeree, "Erik Erikson," 7.

[177] Ibid.

[178] Erikson, *Identity and the Life Cycle*, 91.

[179] Ibid.

[180] Boeree, "Erik Erikson," 8.

[181] Ibid.

[182] Erikson, *Identity and the Life Cycle*, 94.

[183] Boeree, "Erik Erikson," 8-9.

[184] Ibid.

[185] Erikson, *Identity and the Life Cycle*, 100-1.

[186] Boeree, "Erik Erikson," 10.

[187] Ibid.

[188] Ibid.

[189] Ibid.

[190] Erikson, *Identity and the Life Cycle*, 103.

[191] Boeree, "Erik Erikson," 10-11.

[192] Ibid., 11.

[193] Ibid.

[194] Erikson, *Identity and the Life Cycle*, 104.

[195] Ibid.

[196] Boeree, "Erik Erikson," 11-12.

[197] Ibid., 12.

[198] Dr. C. George Boeree, "Abraham Maslow: 1908-1970," *Personality Theories* 2004: 1; available from http://www.ship.edu/~cgboeree/maslow.html; Internet; accessed 8 October 2004.

[199] Ibid.

[200] Ibid.

[201] Ibid.

[202] Ibid.

[203] Betty Dintelman, "Maslow's Hierarchy of Needs," *International Encyclopedia of Justice Studies* December, 2002: 1; available from http://www.iejs.com/Management/maslows_hierarchy_of_needs.htm; Internet; accessed 8 October 2004.

[204] Ibid.

[205] Ibid., 1-2.

[206] Abraham H. Maslow, *Maslow on Management* (New York: John Wiley & Sons, Inc., 1998), 15.

[207] Ibid., xx.

[208] "Maslow's Hierarchy of Needs;" available from http://honolulu.hawaii.edu/intranet/committees/FacDevCom/guidebk/teachtip/maslow.htm; Internet; accessed 8 October 2004.

[209] Robert Gwynne, "Maslow's Hierarchy of Needs," 1997: 1; available from http://web.utk.edu/~gwynne/maslow.HTM; Internet; accessed 8 October 2004.

[210] Abraham H. Maslow, *Maslow on Management*, xx.

[211] Boeree, "Abraham Maslow," 2.

[212] Ibid.

[213] Ibid.

[214] Robert J. Sternberg, *Psychology: In Search of the Human Mind*, Third Edition (New York: Harcourt College Publishers, 2001), 400.

[215] Ibid.

[216] Aileen Milne, *Counselling* (Chicago, Illinois: Contemporary Books, 1999), 151.

[217] Sternberg, *Psychology*, 400.

[218] Ibid.

[219] Milne, *Counselling*, 152.

[220] Abraham H. Maslow, *Toward A Psychology of Being,* Third Edition
    (New York: John Wiley & Sons, Inc., 1999), xiv.

[221] Alan Chapman, "maslow's hierarchy of needs," *businessballs.com*
    2001-4: 1; available from http://www.businessballs.com/
    maslow.htm; Internet; accessed 8 October 2004.

[222] Ibid., 3.

[223] Sternberg, *Psychology: In Search of the Human Mind*, 491.

[224] Roger Fisher, William Ury and Bruce Patton, *Getting to Yes:
    Negotiating Agreement Without Giving In* (New York, New York:
    Penguin Books USA Inc.), 4-5.

[225] Ibid., 10-11.

SELECTED BIBLIOGRAPHY

Barr, Lee and Norma. *The Leadership Equation: Leadership, Management and the Myers-Briggs.* Austin, Texas: Eakin Press, 1989.

Beer, Jennifer, with Eileen Stief. *The Mediator's Handbook.* Canada: New Society Publishers, 1997.

Blackwell, Larry. "Transformative Mediation: A Best Fit for the Workplace." *The CEO Refresher Archives.* 2004. Available from http://www.refresher.com/rbmediation. html; Internet; accessed 19 September 2004.

Boeree, Dr. C. George. "Abraham Maslow: 1908-1970." *Personality Theories.* 2004. Available from http://www.ship.edu/~cgboeree/maslow.html; Internet; accessed 8 October 2004.

_____. "Erik Erikson: 1902 – 1994." *Personality Theories.* 1997. Available from http://www.ship.edu/~cgboeree/erikson.html; Internet; accessed 8 October 2004.

_____. "Sigmund Freud: 1856 – 1939." *Personality Theories.* 1977. Available from http://www.ship.edu/~cgboeree/freud.html; Internet; accessed 8 October 2004.

Breyer, Louis. *Freud: Darkness in the Midst of Vision.* New York: John Wiley & Sons, Inc., 2000.

Bush, Robert A. Baruch, and Joseph P. Folger. *The Promise of Mediation: The Transformative Approach to Conflict.* Revised Edition. San Francisco, CA: Jossey-Bass, 2005.

Chapman, Alan. "maslow's hierarchy of needs."
    Businessballs.com. 2001-4. Available from http://
    www.businessballs.com/maslow.htm; Internet; ac-
    cessed 8 October 2004.

Dintelman, Betty. "Maslow's Hierarchy of Needs." *Inter-*
    national Encyclopaedia of Justice Studies. December
    2002. Available from http://www.iejs.com/Manage-
    ment/ maslows_hierarchy_of_needs.htm; Internet;
    accessed 8 October 2004.

Dundas, Hew R. "Mediation in England: Some Current
    Issues." *Oil, Gas & Energy*. Volume I, issue #02,
    March 2003. Available from http://
    www.gasandoil.com/ogel/samples/ freearticles/
    article_74.htm; Internet; accessed 19 September 2004.

Erikson, Erik H. *Identity and the Life Cycle*. New York: W.
    W. Norton & Company, 1980.

Fisher, Roger, William Ury and Bruce Patton. *Getting to*
    Yes: Negotiating Agreement Without Giving In. New
    York, New York: Penguin Books USA Inc., 1991.

Freud, Sigmund. *Inhibitions, Symptoms and Anxiety*. New
    York: W. W. Norton & Company, 1959.

_____. *The Ego and the Id*. New York: W. W. Norton
    & Company, 1960.

Friedman, Lawrence J. *Identity's Architect: A Biography of*
    Erik H. Erikson. Cambridge, Massachusetts: Harvard
    University Press, 2000.

Gwynne, Robert. "Maslow's Hierarchy of Needs." 1997.
Available from http://web.utk.edu/ ~gwynne/
maslow.HTM; Internet; accessed 8 October 2004.

Hall, Calvin S. *A Primer of Freudian Psychology*. New
York, New York: Meridian, 1999.

Hall, Calvin S., and Vernon J. Nordby. *A Primer of Jungian Psychology*. New York, New York: Meridian,
1999.

Harbaugh, Gary L. *God's Gifted People: Discovering Your
Personality As A Gift*. Expanded ed. Minneapolis,
Minnesota: Augsburg Fortress, 1990.

Harder, MA, MFT, Arlene F. "The Developmental Stages
of Erik Erikson." *Learning Place Online.com*. 2002.
Available from http://www.learningplaceonline.com/
stages/organize/ Erikson.htm; Internet; accessed 8
October 2004.

Jung, C. G. *Memories, Dreams, Reflections*. Edited by
Amiela Jaffe, translated by Richard and Clara Winston. New York: Vantage Books, 1965.

Keirsey, David, and Marilyn Bates. *Please Understand
Me: Character and Temperament Types*. 4th ed. Del
Mar, California: Prometheus Nemesis Book Company,
1984.

Leviton, Sharon C., and James L. Greenstone. *Elements of
Mediation*. Pacific Grove, California: Brooks/Cole
Publishing Company, 1997.

Maslow, Abraham H. *Maslow on Management*. New
York: John Wiley & Sons, Inc., 1998.

_____. *Toward A Psychology of Being*. Third Edition. New York: John Wiley & Sons, Inc., 1999.

"Maslow's Hierarchy of Needs." Available from http:// honolulu.hawaii.edu/intranet/ committees.FacDevCom/guidebk/teachtip/ maslow.htm; Internet; accessed 8 October 2004.

"Mediation." Available from http://www.spea.indiana.edu/ lbingham/v547/ Mediation%20Introduction.htm; Internet; accessed 20 September 2004.

Mediation and Conflict Resolution Office. "Different Types of Mediation Styles." *The Maryland Legal Assistance Network*. 1999-2004. Available from http:// www.peoples_law.org/core/mediation/adr/_directory/ mediation_approaches.htm; Internet; accessed 19 September 2004.

Milne, Aileen. *Counselling*. Chicago, Illinois: Contemporary Books, 1999.

Moore, Christopher W. *The Mediation Process: Practical Strategies for Resolving Conflict*. 3rd Edition Revised. San Francisco, CA: Jossey-Bass, 2003.

Morgan, John H. *Being Human: Perspectives on Meaning and Interpretation*. Bristol, IN: Quill Books, 2002.

Myers, Selma, and Barbara Filmer. "Mediation Concepts." *Conflict Resolution Across Cultures: From Talking It Out to Third Party Mediation*. Available from http:// www. diversityresources.com/rc21d/mediation.html; Internet; accessed 2 January 2004.

Restorative Justice Online. "What Is Restorative Justice?" *Restorative Justice*. 1999. Available from http://www.restorativejustice.org/rj3/intro_default.htm; Internet; accessed 19 September 2004.

Scott, Rob. "The NVMS Approach to Mediation." *Northern Virginia Mediation Service Resolutionary*. 1996-2003. Available from http://www.gmu.edu/departments/nvms/ mediate.htm; Internet; accessed 20 September 2004.

Spangler, Brad. "General Basis and Background of Transformative Mediation." *Transformative Mediation*. 2003. Available from http://www.beyondintractability.org/m/transformative_mediation.jsp; Internet; accessed 19 September 2004.

Sternberg, Robert J. *Psychology: In Search of the Human Mind*. Third Edition. New York: John Wiley & Sons, Inc., 1999.

Storr, Anthony. *Freud*. New York: Barnes & Noble Books, 1998.

Van Ness, Daniel, and Karen Heetderks Strong. *Restoring Justice*. Cincinnati, OH: Anderson Publishing Co., 1997.

Zumeta, J.D., Zena D. "Styles of Mediation: Facilitative, Evaluative and Transformative Mediation." Available from http://learn2mediate.com/resources/nacfm.php; Internet; accessed 4 August 2004.

ABOUT THE AUTHOR

Henry A. Chan was born in Guyana, South America, and migrated to the U.S.A. as a young man in 1967. He worked in information processing in the areas of programming, systems design, systems analysis and long-range planning. Since his ordination to the priesthood in the Episcopal Church in 1983, he has served as a parish priest in the Diocese of Long Island. He holds a B.S. in Computer and Information Science from Empire State College, State University of New York; a M.B.A. in Management from Dowling College; a S.T.M. from the General Theological Seminary; a D.P.A. from Nova Southeastern University; a D.Min. from the School of Theology, University of the South; and a Ph.D. in Pastoral Psychology and a Psy.D. from the Graduate Theological Foundation. He currently serves as a mediator at Community Mediation Services in Jamaica, Queens, New York, where he is a member of the Board of Directors since 2002. He is also a member of the New York State Dispute Resolution Association. Dr. Chan also serves as Professor of Mediation and Pastoral Care at the Graduate Theological Foundation.